A
19th CENTURY RAILWAY
STATION

Series Editor	David Salariya
Book Editor	Hazel Songhurst
Design Assistant	Carol Attwood
Consultant	Tom Richards

Author:

Fiona Macdonald studied history at Cambridge University and at the University of East Anglia. She has taught children, adults and undergraduates. She has written many books on historical topics, mainly for children.

Illustrator:

John James was born in London in 1959. He studied at Eastbourne College of Art and has specialized in historical reconstruction since leaving art school in 1982.

Consultant:

Tom Richards joined the Great Western Railway as a lad clerk at his home town of St. Ives, Cornwall and worked his way up through the system to management positions in the operating and planning departments. He retired in 1982 as a Senior Officer, Western Region at Paddington Headquarters. Since then, he has compiled a directory of railway staff archive sources for family historians.

© The Salariya Book Co Ltd 1990

First American edition published in 1990 by
Peter Bedrick Books
2112 Broadway
New York, NY 10023

Library of Congress Cataloging-in-Publication Data
Macdonald, Fiona.
   A 19th century railway station / Fiona Macdonald ; John James—
—1st American ed.
      p.   cm.
   Summary: Text and illustrations describe the planning, construction, and activities of a nineteenth-century railway station.
   ISBN 0-87226-341-X
   1. Railroads—Stations—Juvenile literature. [1. Railroads—Stations.]
I. John James. II. Title. III. Title: Nineteenth century railway station.
TF300.M33   1990
385'.314' 09034—dc20   90-36254
                                                                      CIP
                                                                      AC
Printed in Great Britain
90 91 92 93 94 5 4 3 2 1

A
19th CENTURY RAILWAY
STATION

FIONA MACDONALD   JOHN JAMES

PETER BEDRICK BOOKS
NEW YORK

CONTENTS

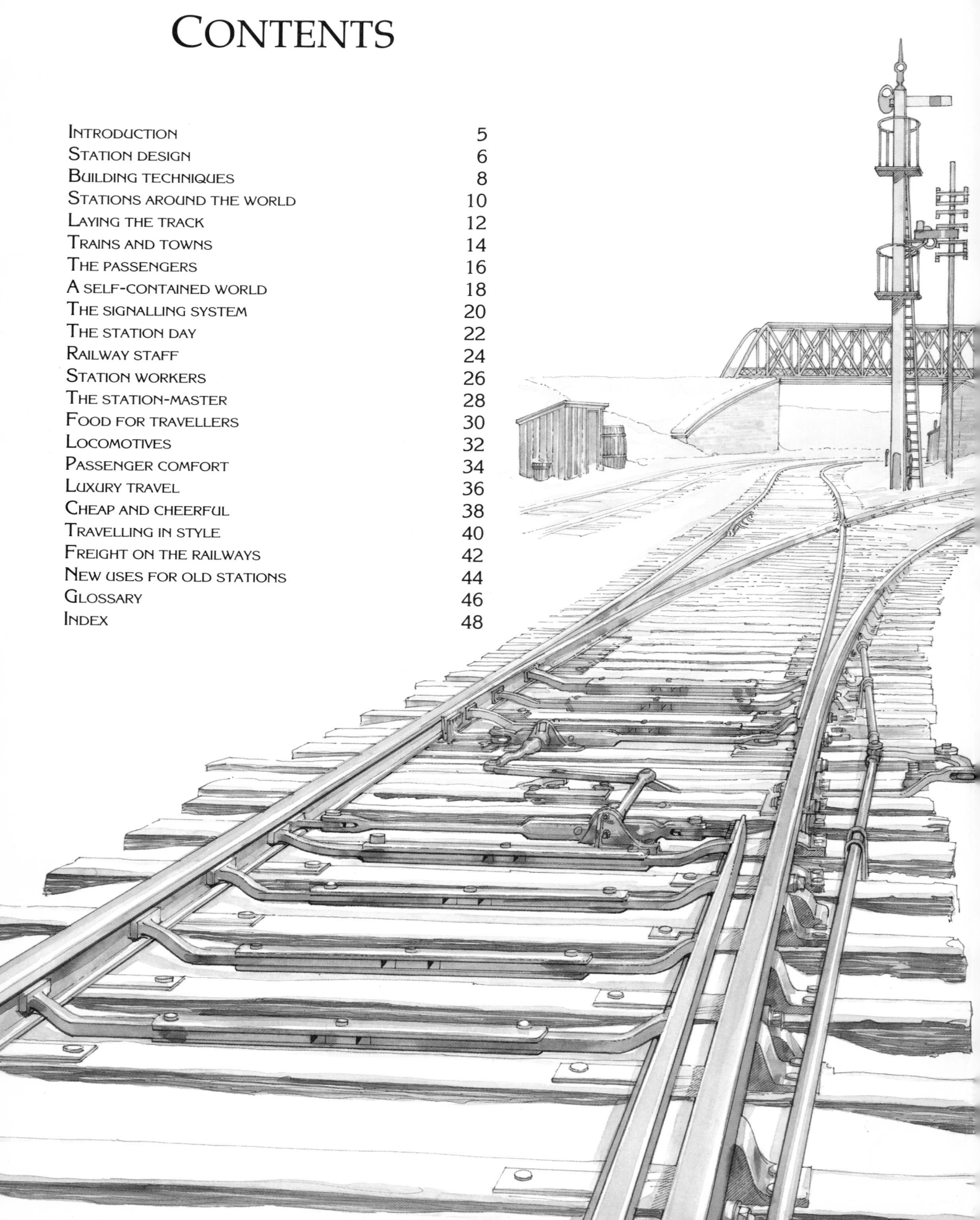

INTRODUCTION

Railways have been called 'the greatest revolution in transport since the invention of the wheel'. Certainly, in the years which followed the first successful trials of a steam passenger locomotive in 1830, it became possible for goods and people to travel further and faster than ever before.

Railways enabled new industries to develop, new cities to grow and new continents to be opened up. They encouraged people to commute from leafy suburbs to work in crowded towns, and allowed exhausted city-dwellers to seek relaxation in far-away holiday resorts. They carried wholesome farm produce to customers in towns, and brought city fashions, new manufactured goods, and the latest national news to isolated villages. They transported raw materials for industry from distant mines and mills, and ferried the finished products to the ports.

In many towns and cities, we can still see huge railways stations, built over 100 years ago to cater to the new railways and their passengers. This book will help you find out more about these great 19th-century stations — how they were designed and built, how they were run — and about the lives of the people who worked in them.

STATION DESIGN

Crane winching up iron girders

Iron rafters

Wood

Site foreman

Architect

Pediments

This illustration shows a railway station under construction in the 1840s. The architect has copied building styles which were fashionable in ancient Greece and Rome.

Look at the rounded arches, the colonnade (like a porch, designed to shelter passengers as they descended from their horse-drawn carriages), and the pediments (decorative tops) to the windows. They have all been copied from Roman villas and temples.

The earliest railway stations were simple buildings; the first ever, at Liverpool Road in Manchester, consisted of just a few open platforms where passengers waited to board their trains. Later, roofs were added, along with ticket offices, waiting rooms and storage space for goods.

Railway architects in the 19th century had no earlier buildings to use as models – there had been no need for stations before passenger locomotives were invented. The architects' task was to design stations that were spacious enough to accommodate steamy, smoky engines, long strings of coaches, crowds of passengers, stacks of freight and the railway staff, all at once. The new stations had to be quick and easy to erect, pleasant and comfortable to work or wait in, and impressive enough to attract new passengers.

Who paid for these massive station buildings? Mostly private investors, although in some European countries governments offered financial help to develop new routes. Independent railway companies were set up, and shares were sold in them to raise the money needed to build stations, locomotives and tracks. Investors hoped that their shares would increase in value as the railway company prospered, and this was what usually happened. If the company made a profit, then that would be paid back to the investors as well.

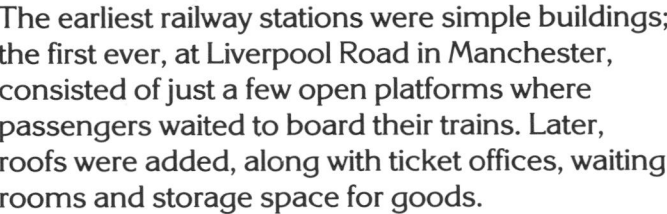

Stucco

Colonnade

Here we can see workmen on the station roof (left), and covering the brickwork with stucco, a plaster-based mixture (right). Although many of the building components, in particular the iron pillars and rafters, were factory-made, 19th-century stations still relied on the strength and skill of the labourers who built them, and on traditional materials, like wood, for doors, floors and windows.

Architects, surveyors and railway managers all demanded high standards of craftsmanship from their workers, as well as good-quality materials. We can see, from the many examples that survive today, that 19th-century railway stations were very solidly built. Hundreds of men were employed in building a large station; when complete, it would also need many maintenance workers to keep it clean and in good repair.

The railways were one of the greatest achievements of the industrial revolution that transformed Britain, America and Europe in the 19th century.

BUILDING TECHNIQUES

Stations built in the 19th century had towering walls, soaring, wide-span roofs and high, vaulted ceilings. Most were built very quickly, and were ready for use by trains and passengers within 5–10 years. How were these remarkable feats of engineering achieved?

Railway architects used the most up-to-date techniques to construct their stations. New materials, such as cast iron, mild steel and plate glass, enabled them to build quickly, and on a vast scale. A typical station might have walls built round a framework of cast-iron pillars and arches, supporting a roof made of iron ribs, covered by sheets of glass fixed to mild steel bars. All these components could be mass-produced cheaply in factories, then fitted together easily on site. It was a far quicker method than building in brick or stone, where load-bearing walls and roof trusses had to be constructed laboriously by hand.

These new building methods produced lighter structures than traditional materials, which meant that architects could design very large buildings that were also safe and strong. A glass roof weighed much less than one covered with slates or tiles; it was therefore more suitable for roofing a large area. Glass also let in the daylight; this made stations pleasant to work in, and, since less artificial lighting was required, cheaper to run.

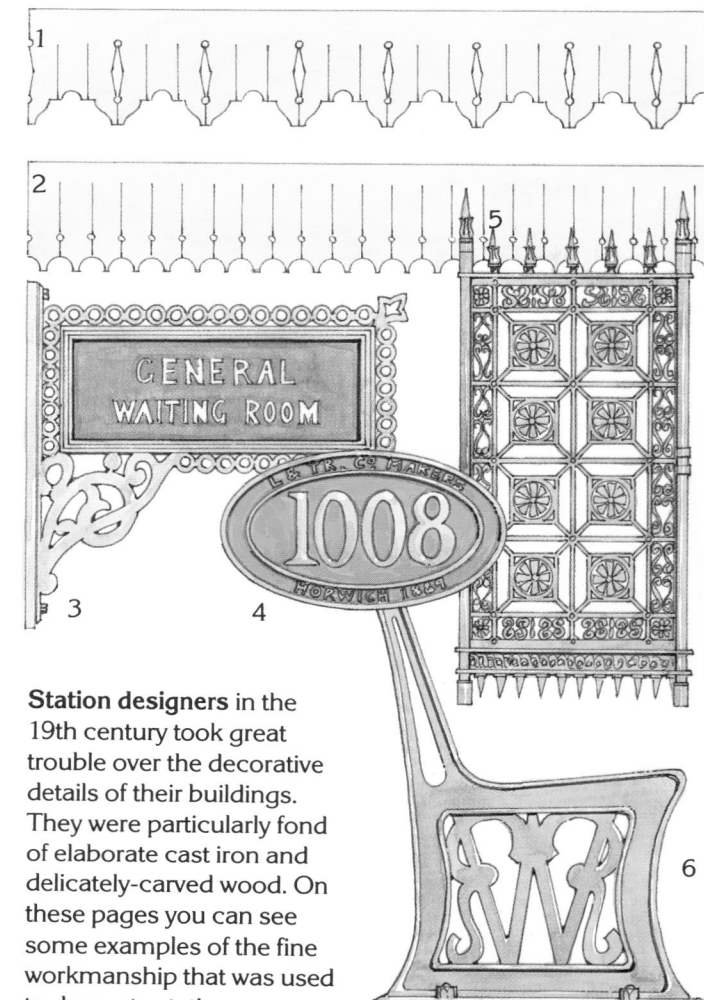

Station designers in the 19th century took great trouble over the decorative details of their buildings. They were particularly fond of elaborate cast iron and delicately-carved wood. On these pages you can see some examples of the fine workmanship that was used to decorate stations.

Decorative details
1 and 2. Wooden valances for station roofs.
3. Ornamental sign.
4. Locomotive number plate.
5. Wrought-iron gate.
6. Decorative initials, 'GWR'.
7. Timber-clad station.
8. Ironwork canopy supports.
9. Arched roof supports.
10. Fine iron-work .
11. Ornamental column.
12. Carved wooden pillars.
13. Elaborate cast-iron 'classical style' decoration.
14. Ironwork window.

Arches, roofs, pillars and even seats were made of iron cast into fantastic shapes, often copied from earlier buildings, such as palaces, castles and cathedrals. Sometimes, the railway company's initials were worked into the elaborate design.

On other occasions, designers looked to distant lands for inspiration, and copied Greek temples, Roman monuments or even Russian summerhouses. Other designs were based on fruit, flowers and abstract geometric patterns all jumbled together.

STATIONS AROUND THE WORLD

Wherever railways were developed, stations had also to be built, to provide facilities for passengers and staff. But even though they all had to fulfil the same functions, few 19th-century railway stations resembled one another. What prompted architects to build these new stations in so many weird and wonderful styles?

Some stations were designed to impress. If the station building looked strong and secure, then travellers felt safe. And people with money to invest in a railway company might be reassured by a solid, prosperous-looking building. Fashion also had a part to play: during the 19th century, houses, furniture, carpets and curtains were often decorated with designs copied from the past, or borrowed from distant, exotic cultures. Following this trend, stations were built to resemble medieval churches or mountain chalets, however odd they might look in their new surroundings.

Small, suburban stations were designed to blend in with neighbouring buildings: many of them even had gardens, and might easily be mistaken for a comfortable family home. Country stations looked like farmhouses or cottages.

But, on the whole, 19th-century railway stations reflected the confidence and exuberance of the men who designed and built them. The railway pioneers were rich, successful, energetic and highly individual. They built to please themselves.

1   Fenny Stratford Station, Buckinghamshire

2   St Pancras Station, London

3   Union Station, St Louis, USA

4   Old Churchgate Station, India

Munich Station, Germany

A variety of styles

1. Suburban station at Fenny Stratford, Buckinghamshire, UK. Built in the late 19th century, to match the new houses surrounding it.

2. St Pancras Station and Hotel, London. Designed by Gilbert Scott and built during the 1860s. It resembles a great medieval cathedral, with lofty towers, steep roofs and pointed windows.

3. The Union Station at St Louis, Missouri, designed and built during the 1890s. Some of its features, like the rounded corner towers, became very popular in the American Mid-West.

4. Old Churchgate Station on the Bombay, Baroda and Central Indian Railway. Often, railway stations in India developed into bazaars, where goods were bought and sold. In remote districts, trains were infrequent; people might have to wait two or three days for one. Poor passengers spent this time on the platform – eating, sleeping and washing in the open air.

5. The first station in Munich, in the German state of Bavaria. It was designed by Friedrich Burklein in 1849, in a mixture of international and local styles. The doors and windows would not look out of place on any 19th-century public building, but the carved wooden boards under the eaves are copied from local village houses.

LAYING THE TRACK

In 1840, there were only about 6,250 mi of track worldwide (most of it in England, Belgium and the USA), but by 1900, there were almost 500,000 mi (about 172,000 mi in Europe, 225,000 mi in the USA, and the rest spread through many other lands). Building a new railway track was extremely hard work. First the land had to be surveyed, to find the best route for the railway to follow. Trains ran most efficiently on straight, level tracks; sharp bends or steep downhill runs were dangerous; long uphill climbs were slow and wasted fuel.

Where possible, new routes were laid out to bypass obstacles, but they could not always be avoided. Bridges were built to cross rivers and estuaries, tunnels and cuttings were blasted through rocky hillsides, and embankments carried the track above marshy or steeply-sloping ground.

The men who built the railways were rough and tough. They spent all day in backbreaking physical labour, and slept in camps alongside the tracks at night. They worked in gangs, and were fiercely loyal to their mates, but disrespectful of almost everyone else. They were well paid, but their work was extremely dangerous. Over 100 men were killed building the London to Bristol stretch of the Great Western Railway (a distance of about 100 mi). It is hardly surprising that the workers on the Union Pacific Railroad in the USA called the track train that took them to work 'hell on wheels'.

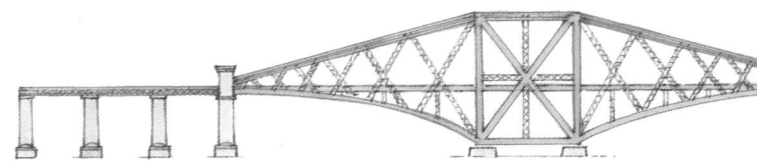

1 Forth Rail Bridge

2 Primrose Hill Tunnel

3 Torrington Truss Bridge, USA.

4

Tunnel, Great Western Railway

5. (Left) The Schurrtobel Bridge on the Vitznau-Rigi Railway in Switzerland, built in 1870. The rack-and-pinion track runs through mountainous countryside and across deep ravines.

The Schurrtobel Bridge, Switzerland

5

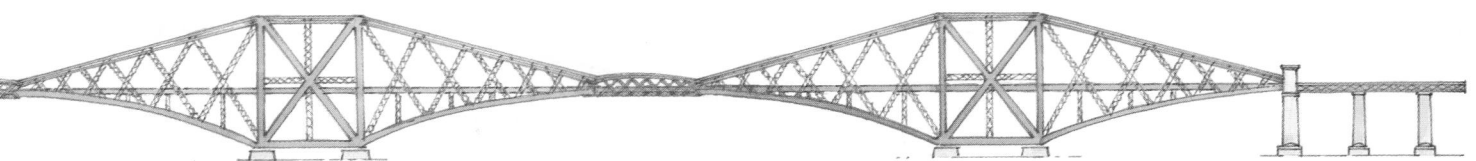

1. The Forth Rail Bridge, which spans the estuary of the River Forth in Scotland, was designed by Sir John Fowler and Benjamin Baker, and opened in 1890. The bridge is based on the cantilever principle: three enormous diamond-shaped structures support the railway suspended between them. It is built of steel girders, resting on huge cylindrical piers cemented into the seabed.

2. Primrose Hill Tunnel, on the London to Birmingham Line. Cutting tunnels through solid rock, or unstable clay, was both difficult and dangerous.

3. The Torrington Truss Bridge, Nangatuck, New Haven and Hartford, New York State, USA. A bridge made of strong, cross-braced steel girders, or trusses. This metal bridge replaced an earlier wooden structure. Metal was stronger than wood and was fire-resistant. Even so, many early American railway bridges were made of wood, since they were quicker, easier and cheaper to build.

4. The entrance to a 'box' tunnel on the Great Western Railway, near Bath. This line was constructed by the famous engineer, Isambard Kingdom Brunel, between 1835 and 1841.

Labourers laying new track in a vast tunnel blasted through a hillside. The opening in the tunnel roof lets in ventilation and light for the gang to work by as well as providing access for tools and materials.

TRAINS AND TOWNS

In the 19th century, towns and railways grew together. Towns expanded as their new mass-production industries flourished. All manner of buildings – warehouses, factories, breweries, gasworks – were erected alongside the railway tracks, so that it was easy to load their raw materials and finished products. And millions of new houses were built for the workers who flocked to the towns in search of employment. Trains brought the building materials – bricks, glass, slates and iron – to construct these new factories and houses, and food to feed the workers.

By the 1860s, most important towns had a station. Some towns, situated on routes operated by competing railway companies, ended up with two or even three rival stations. These stations brought many changes to the towns they served. They were vast: their platforms, offices, entrance yards, booking halls, engine sheds, sidings and goods storage yards occupied large tracts of land.

There were other buildings associated with the railway, too. There might be a station hotel, built by the railway company to provide accommodation for travellers, and houses of varying size and splendour for all the railway staff. These ranged from the station master's grand villa to rows of little terraced houses for the porters and guards.

Viaducts were built to carry railway tracks above ground that was sloping or otherwise unsuitable. Roman engineers used viaducts to carry military roads; 19th-century railway builders found a new use for this old invention.

Goods yards and engine sheds were built alongside passenger stations. They provided space where bulky goods could be unloaded from rail wagons to horse-drawn carts. Sheds also provided shelter for valuable locomotives.

Viaduct

Engine sheds

Turntables (sections of track that could be swung round in a circle) allowed locomotives to be turned right round. They were essential at the end of railway lines. Without them, locomotives would be forced to make their return journey backwards.

Signal-boxes housed the levers needed for working signals which guided the trains. A signalman's job was very responsible; a mistake could lead to disaster. The signals, below right, are in the horizontal position, which means 'line not clear'.

Locomotives, trucks and carriages needed regular servicing, and so most stations were built with workshops. There was also space for track maintenance workers to store the materials they needed – rails, sleepers, sand and ballast.

Station hotel

Station

Sidings

Signal box

Turntable

Signals

THE PASSENGERS

Passengers travelled with a great deal of luggage. Here we can see trunks of various shapes and sizes, crates and holdalls. Trunks were usually made of wood covered with leather, although for travel to tropical countries where ants and termites might be a problem, they were made of metal. Goods in transit might also be packed in wicker baskets. These provided some protection against knocks and jolts on the journey, but wore out quickly. They were cheap to replace however, and much lighter to carry than passengers' heavy trunks.

High-class luggage was fitted-out with removable trays and drawers for different items of clothing.

A well-made trunk was very expensive, but would last a lifetime. Wealthy women also travelled with drum-shaped hatboxes, which were beautifully padded inside to protect their hats — fragile confections of velvet, ribbons, lace or straw.

Who travelled by train in the 19th century? Almost everybody, from kings, queens and presidents to poor migrants on their way to the docks in search of a better life in another land.

The first rail passengers were usually nervous as they boarded their trains. This was hardly surprising; early locomotives were terrifying machines. They belched smoke and sparks, their funnels glowed red-hot, they seemed always on the point of exploding. Accidents did happen; in 1830, the first successful American steam engine blew up after only 6 months in service. In France, one railway company arranged for the Bishop of Paris to bless the first train that ran on the new line between Rouen and Le Havre, to calm public fears.

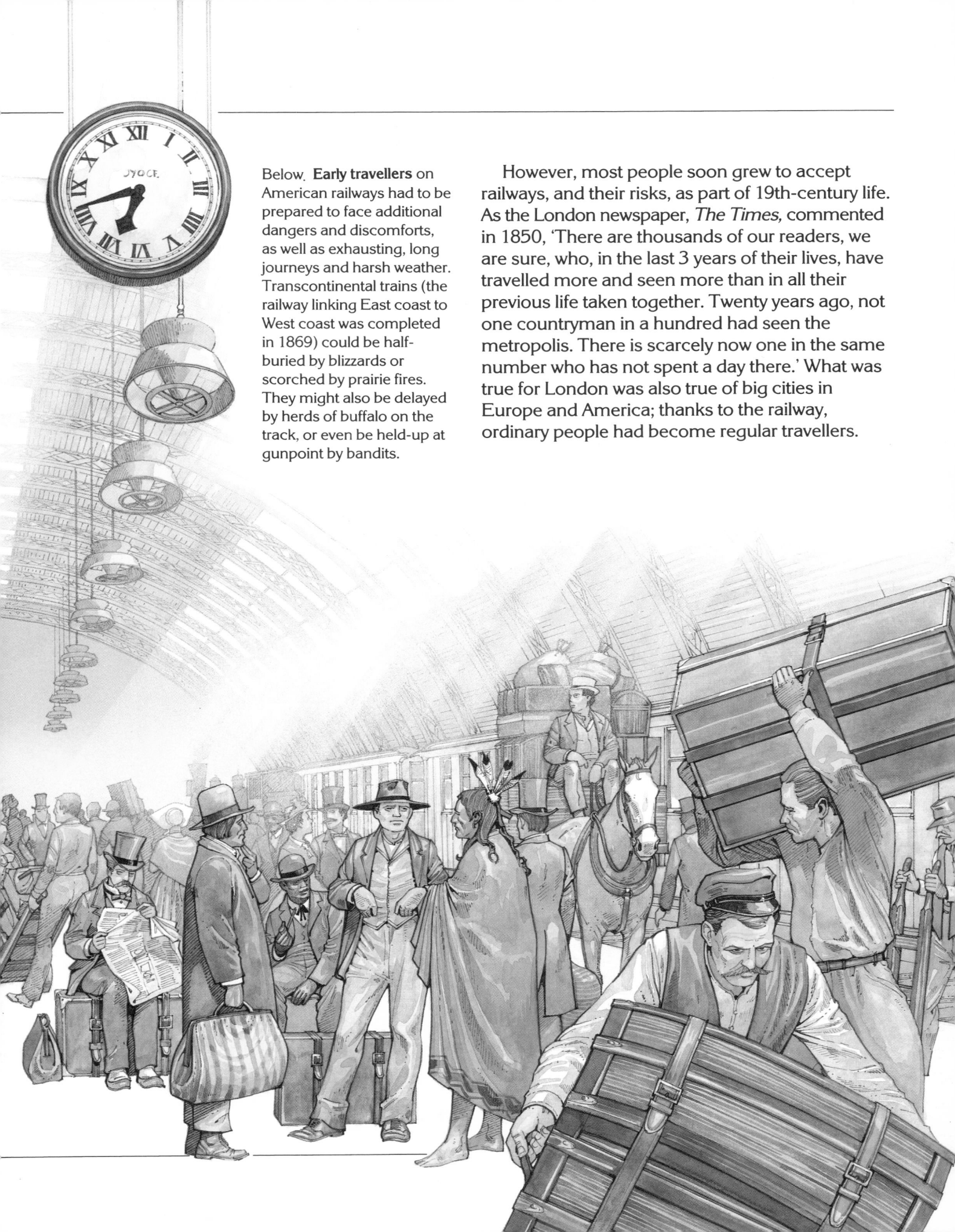

Below. **Early travellers** on American railways had to be prepared to face additional dangers and discomforts, as well as exhausting, long journeys and harsh weather. Transcontinental trains (the railway linking East coast to West coast was completed in 1869) could be half-buried by blizzards or scorched by prairie fires. They might also be delayed by herds of buffalo on the track, or even be held-up at gunpoint by bandits.

However, most people soon grew to accept railways, and their risks, as part of 19th-century life. As the London newspaper, *The Times,* commented in 1850, 'There are thousands of our readers, we are sure, who, in the last 3 years of their lives, have travelled more and seen more than in all their previous life taken together. Twenty years ago, not one countryman in a hundred had seen the metropolis. There is scarcely now one in the same number who has not spent a day there.' What was true for London was also true of big cities in Europe and America; thanks to the railway, ordinary people had become regular travellers.

A SELF-CONTAINED WORLD

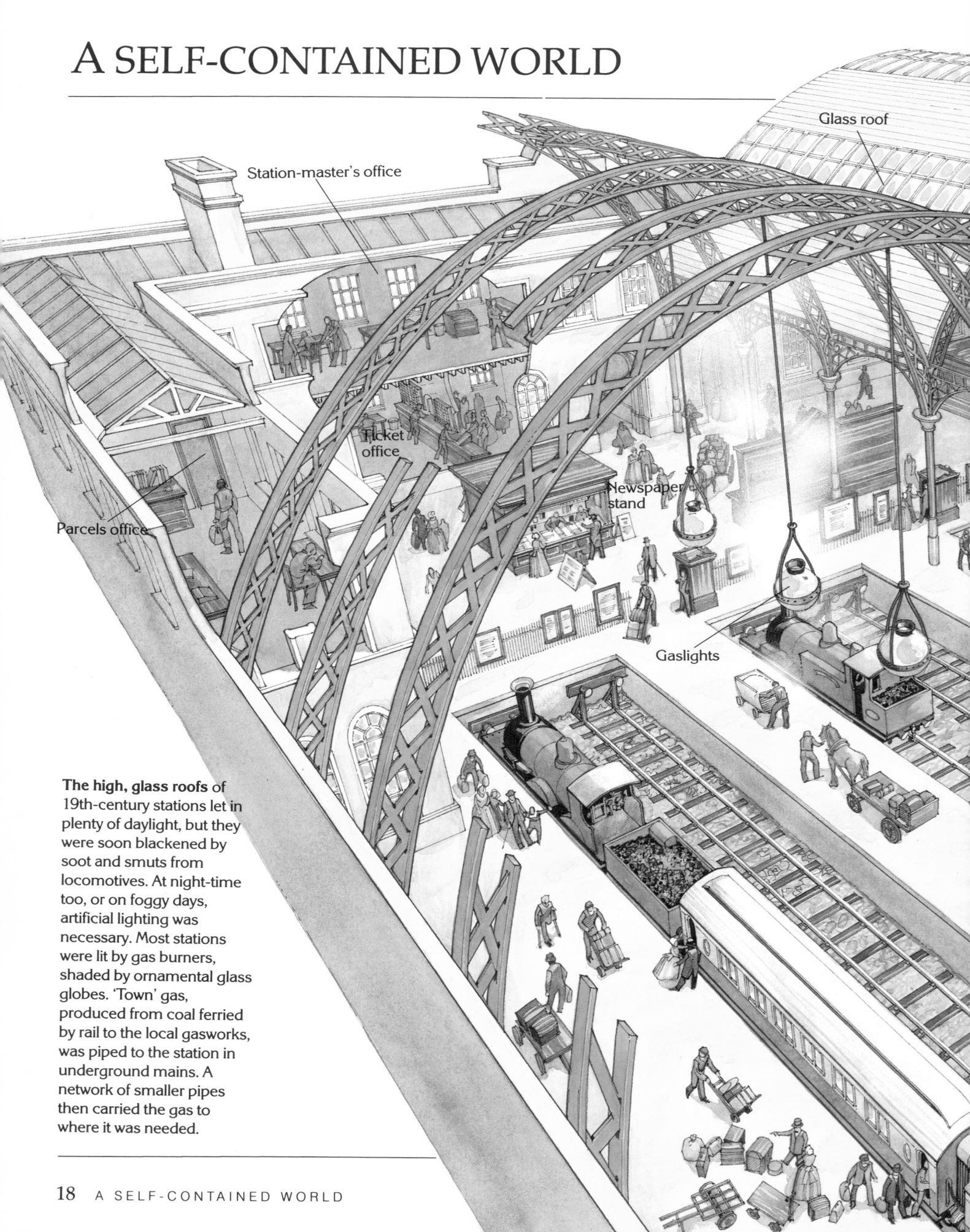

Station-master's office

Glass roof

Ticket office

Parcels office

Newspaper stand

Gaslights

The high, glass roofs of 19th-century stations let in plenty of daylight, but they were soon blackened by soot and smuts from locomotives. At night-time too, or on foggy days, artificial lighting was necessary. Most stations were lit by gas burners, shaded by ornamental glass globes. 'Town' gas, produced from coal ferried by rail to the local gasworks, was piped to the station in underground mains. A network of smaller pipes then carried the gas to where it was needed.

Luggage checkroom

Waiting room

Lost property office

Rapid rail transport enabled letters and parcels to be delivered much more quickly than in the days of horse-drawn mail coaches. Many stations had rooms set aside for handling mail. Newspapers and magazines were also sent by rail from printing works in major cities. In the days before radio and television, people relied on newspapers to tell them what was going on in the world. In the 19th century, news travelled much faster by train!

Entering a great station was like stepping inside another world. Under the wide-arching glass roof, travellers encountered a maze of offices, drafty platforms and loading bays, and a confusing babble of noise. The hiss of steam mingled with the roar of engines, the shouts of porters, and the cries of hawkers selling their wares.

In his office high above the platforms, the station-master and his assistants arranged duty rosters for staff, received important visitors, and listened to complaints from the public. It was their responsibility to see that everything ran smoothly, from introducing a complicated international timetable to checking the daily cleaning of the platforms and waiting rooms.

Other offices were set aside for selling tickets, handling parcels and sorting mail. There were rest rooms for railway staff, waiting rooms for passengers, public lavatories, a luggage check room, a lost-property store, dining rooms and bars, and a bookstall, selling newspapers and magazines to travellers. There might be vendors selling fruit or flowers, and a host of 'unofficial' workers, trying to earn a living by running messages, cleaning shoes, fetching cabs, or holding parcels and umbrellas while passengers went in search of a meal. In big city stations, travellers might see beggars, homeless people, prostitutes and pickpockets.

Carts were used to carry goods to and from the station. Many stations had a cab-rank outside, where drivers would wait with their horse-drawn cabs ready to meet passengers.

At busy times the station atmosphere could become very dirty and smoky. Waiting passengers often found themselves covered with specks of soot or greasy black smuts.

THE SIGNALLING SYSTEM

Rail traffic along the tracks was controlled by signals, painted wooden arms at the tops of tall poles. They could be moved into a number of positions to indicate 'go', 'proceed with caution' or 'stop'. Locomotive drivers kept watch from their cabs for signals telling them about the track ahead; there were different sets of signals for near or distant lines. At night, signals were given by coloured lamps, fixed to the signal arms.

Signalmen were chosen and trained from among the most intelligent young men who applied for a job on the railways. As well as keeping an eye on all the trains passing through 'their' section of the track, they had to react quickly to urgent messages; there might be a special train coming through, or an accident on the line.

1. Semaphore signals at the entrance to a busy station. The top signals are set in the 'stop' position; the lower signals, known as 'calling on' signals, told drivers whether a platform was free. These signals indicate that the platform is occupied, but that the driver can proceed with caution into the station.

2. Layout of the tracks at the original Paddington Station in 1845. This station was the London terminus of the Great Western Railway, which began in Bristol.

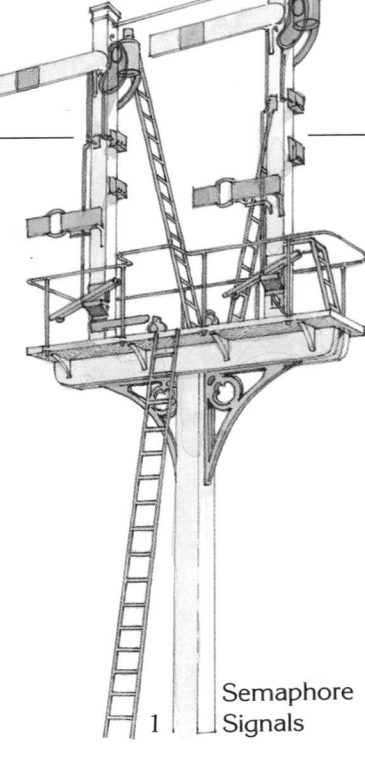

Semaphore
1 Signals

3. Signalmen received messages from stations and other signal-boxes in Morse code, and by electric bells. They also used patent message-sending devices, such as 'Spagnoletti's Block Instrument', shown here.

4. Points fitted with detector bars and switch locks.

5. Level-crossing barrier on an American country road.

6. Flanged wheels, used on locomotives, trucks and passenger carriages. The flange (or rim) helps to keep the wheel on the track. Early railways were built with flanged rails, not wheels, but by the 1850s flanged wheels were standard.

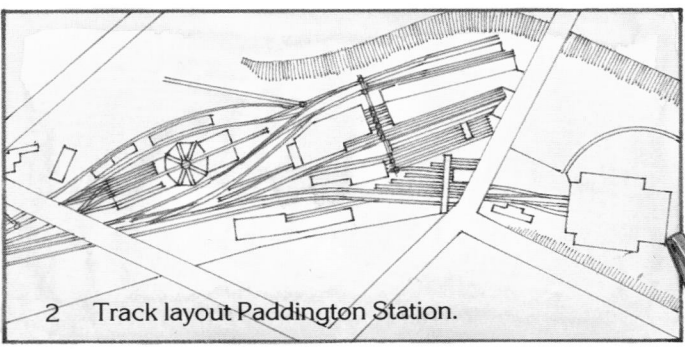

2   Track layout Paddington Station.

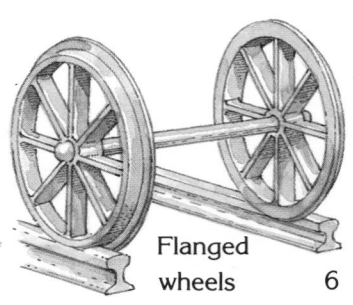

Flanged
wheels   6

4 Points

5 Level-crossing

Signals were controlled from signal boxes, built at the entrance to stations or at key points along the track. Inside were maps of the railway lines, timetables, bells and rows of heavy levers. The levers controlled wires which moved the signal arms. They also controlled sets of points. By the 1890s, signals and points were connected so they could only be moved in unison. Previously, accidents had happened when signals had given the wrong information about how points were set, and had sent two trains hurtling along the same line. Other safety inventions included detector bars, which prevented points being moved while a train was still crossing over them.

7. A signal-box lever, c.1900. Levers were connected to semaphore signals hundreds of metres away by wires running beside the track. The signalman had to move the levers to work the signals.

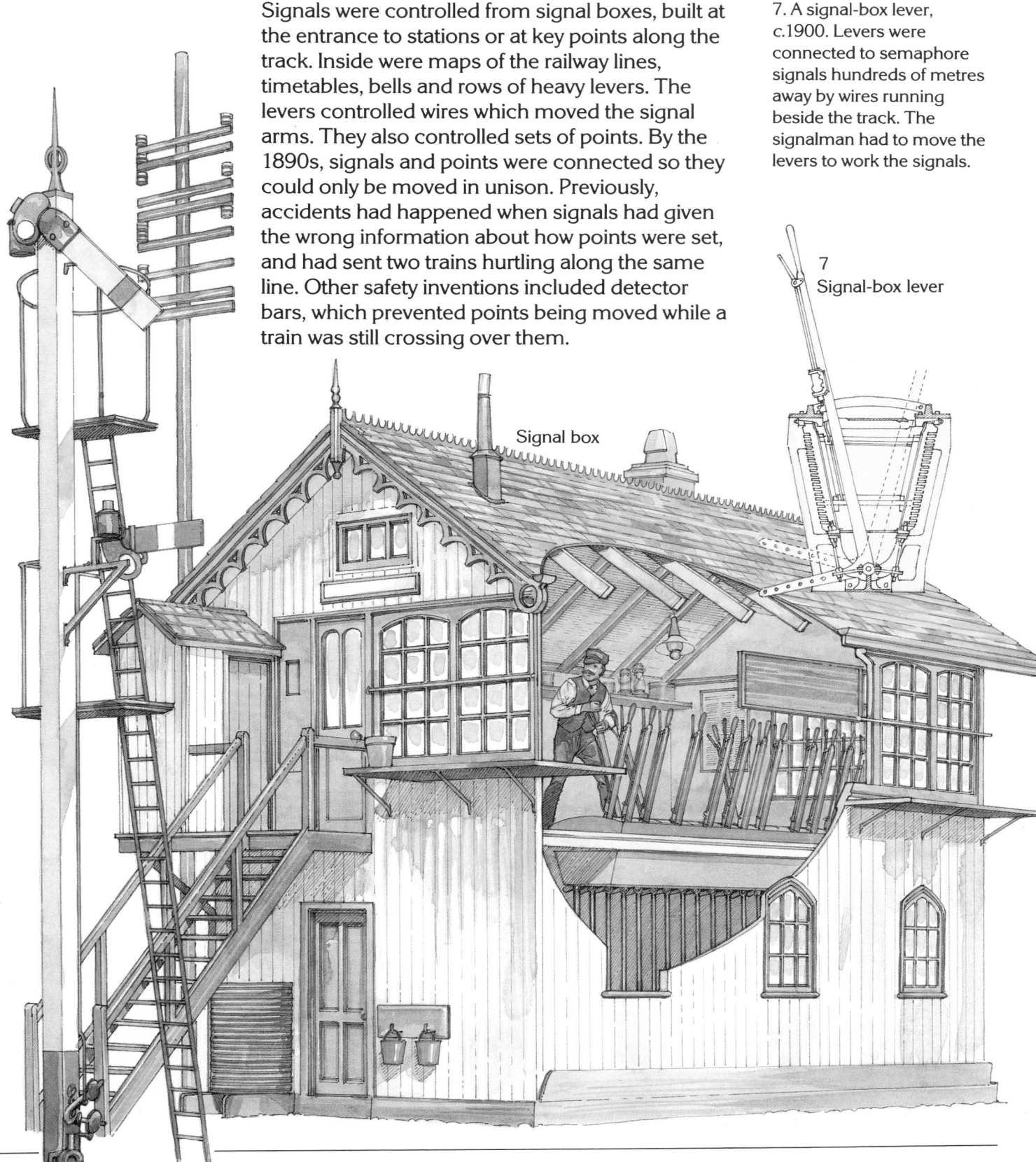

Signal box

7
Signal-box lever

THE STATION DAY

Railway work began very early, long before most passengers were out of bed. Station cleaners were busy, sweeping the platforms, collecting litter, dusting offices and polishing the large expanses of wood and brass used in all the station furniture. Deliveries of bread, milk, meat and vegetables arrived, and were checked for freshness and quality by cooks in the station restaurants. Drivers, guards, ticket collectors and clerks reported for duty; in the sidings, shunters and maintenance men were already hard at work. And no-one knew when the station-master might call in on the way to his office, to carry out a lightning inspection of the staff, and check on what they were doing.

1. The view from inside a ticket office. Passengers purchased their tickets and spoke to the booking clerk through a little window. Tickets were made of card. Different colours showed whether the ticket was 1st, 2nd or 3rd class, and whether it was a single or return. British 3rd-class travel was a penny a mile in the late 1880s.

2. In between journeys, a locomotive might need attention; here the wheels are being oiled, cleaned and checked. While waiting at the station, locomotive boilers also had to be refilled with water, and tenders (the separate truck that ran behind many locomotives to carry the fuel) had to be refilled with wood or coal.

Porters

3

Mornings and evenings were the busiest times for the great stations. Office workers struggled on and off crowded commuter trains, all in a hurry to get to their offices on time, or back home again. Long-distance expresses came and went at all hours of the day and night; their passengers were often accompanied by friends or relatives coming to wave them goodbye. They got in the way of the porters struggling to load the heavy trunks and boxes in time. After dark, the work of marshalling trains, dealing with passengers and unloading goods continued in the glare of gas lamps. The lamps were only extinguished when it was finally time for the station to close for the night.

3. Broad Street Station, Philadelphia, USA, in 1885, showing the recently installed barriers across entrances to the platforms. Now, passengers had to show their tickets to station staff as they boarded or left the train.

4. The elegant tea room on platform 8 of the North Eastern Railway's station at York, c.1910. Potted palms, 'modern' furniture, and even carpets provided pleasant surroundings for waiting passengers. Tea was served by waitresses.

5. A station maintenance worker changes the mantle (the tube around the gas jet) in a lamp. At night, the lamps had to remain lit until the station finally closed.

Working by lamplight

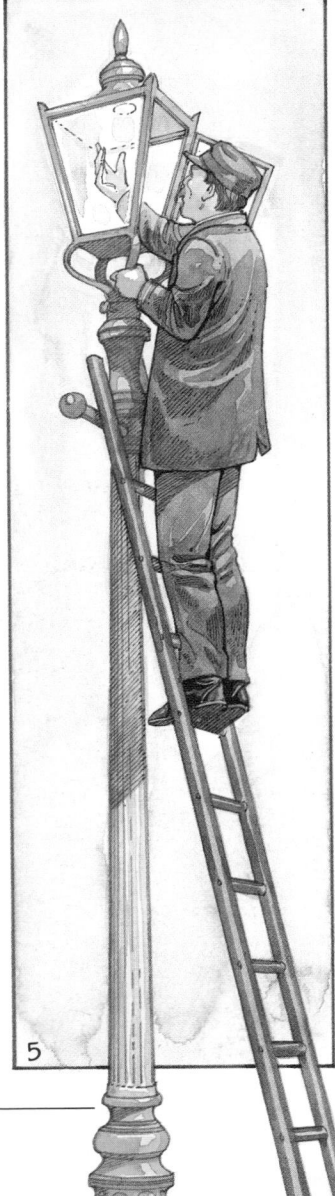

5

4

RAILWAY STAFF

How many passengers who travelled by train gave any thought to the people who kept the railways running? There were two main groups of railway workers; those who drove and cared for the trains, and those who were employed in the stations.

Locomotive drivers were responsible for the safety of a whole trainload of passengers. As well as 'driving' the locomotive, by maintaining the correct speed, working the brakes and looking out for signals, drivers also had to inspect each train in the yard before it set out, to make sure that it was in good working order.

Working on the railways was a way of life and railway staff tended to be fiercely loyal to 'their' company, even though their working conditions were not very good. There were occasional disputes, and some construction workers in remote territories were badly treated. Many died building railway lines in the harsh conditions of the Rocky Mountains.

Station-master

Shunter

Porter

Railway companies provided uniforms for their employees to wear. Like all uniforms, a railway worker's clothing displayed the rank and occupation of its wearer, from the morning suit and silk hat of the station-master to the rough jackets and overalls worn by the shunters and cleaners. Railway workers, whose jobs involved meeting the public, were expected to look smart, to create a good image for their company.

Below. **Passengers** and railway workers setting off on a journey. The station-master (in silk hat) discusses a last-minute problem. The driver has checked the locomotive's supplies of coal, oil and water, and the fireman has built up a good head of steam in the boiler. Porters are struggling with heavy trunks. The fruit seller hopes the passengers will buy some of her oranges to eat on the journey.

Driving a train was demanding work, and the most experienced drivers were proud of their skills. Yet the conditions in which drivers and their assistants (known as firemen) were expected to work were appalling by modern standards. Their cabs were horribly noisy and cramped, and open to the weather. Drivers and firemen were showered with soot, scorched by the heat of the fire-box and chilled by driving sleet and snow. In many cabs, seats were not provided until the 1920s – the driver might have to stand for a journey of over 190 mi. On a similar trip, the fireman would need to shovel over 3 tons of coal, as well as keep a constant watch on the steam pressure level: if it dropped too low, the train would lose speed; if it rose too high, the boiler might explode!

Engine driver

Fireman

Fruit seller

Maintenance man

Porter

STATION WORKERS

At the height of their popularity, railways provided employment for millions of people. Rolling stock was built and maintained by the railway company's mechanics and engineers. They hammered, welded and riveted the heavy iron plates from which trucks and locomotives were made. Carriages were finished at special coachworks, where carpenters and upholsterers added doors, windows, panelling and seating.

Trains were made ready for use by shunters, who crawled beneath the coaches to hitch them together. Engines and rolling stock were washed and swept by gangs of cleaners, who often worked at night. Stations, too, had to be kept clean.

The guard made sure that all passengers were safely on board, and all doors firmly closed, before giving the signal to depart, by flag or whistle. It was his responsibility to make sure that the train left on time. Passengers purchased their tickets from booking clerks; they were checked by ticket-inspectors (or conductors) at various points along the route, and handed in to ticket collectors at the end of the journey. On long-distance trains, passengers were looked after by dining-car and sleeping-car attendants (both first introduced in the USA in the 1860s). The smooth running of the railways depended on the hard work and skills of a great many people.

Soldiers

Newspaper seller

Match seller

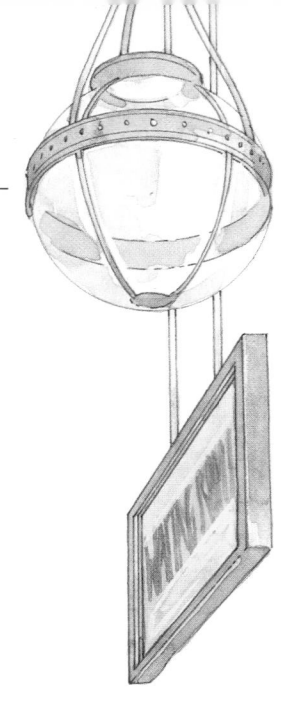

This station platform is crowded with people, but not all of them are travellers. There is a newspaper seller, a little boy selling matches, the train guard, as well as several porters. All these people made their living by working at the station, although the newspaper-seller and match-boy will be lucky to earn more than a few cents a day. Passengers might also see beggars, sheltering in the warmth of the station.

Travellers paid porters to look after their luggage for them. In the earliest trains, luggage had been placed in racks outside on the roof, but by the 1860s, luggage travelled inside, in a separate van, and was looked after by railway staff. The porters had to be strong to lift the heavy trunks and skilled in the art of stacking the luggage in the van, in such a way that it did not fall over and damage the contents.

Look at the clothes of the travellers here. The men wear well-tailored, but rather stiff coats and trousers, with high collars and tall hats (1st-class compartments were fitted with special racks designed to hold top-hats). The women are dressed in voluminous skirts held out by layers of petticoats, tight bodices, flowing cloaks, and bonnets. These were not particularly comfortable clothes in which to travel.

Train guard

Porter

THE STATION-MASTER

A station-master was an important person, doing a useful job. Of course, his responsibilities varied with the size of the station he managed, but everywhere the station-master would be in charge of a large workforce, as well as of valuable buildings, locomotives and signalling equipment. A typical station-master was middle-aged by the time he was considered experienced enough for the task. He would have held a number of junior posts in his company, and know the workings of his local railway system inside out. He needed to be shrewd, quick-thinking and tactful, to deal with staff problems, or soothe disgruntled passengers.

1

Many railway companies provided accommodation for their employees, including the station-master. He was given a comfortable, spacious house, large enough for his family and servants, probably built at the same time as the station, and maybe standing in a pleasant garden. It was usually within walking distance of the station, or at most only a short carriage drive away.

2

3

4

5

The station-master's day

1. Breakfast at home.

2. Setting off for the station. On his way to work, the station-master might pass rows of cottages, built by the railway company to house other railway workers.

3. Arriving at his office. 19th-century offices were often elaborately furnished. In the background, you can see a decorative plaque commemorating a famous railway pioneer.

4. Inspecting a new indicator board, which told passengers where to catch their trains. Before these boards were introduced, passengers had to ask railway staff for information. One guard complained that this 'worried [them] almost to distraction'.

5. Receiving a report on how a new locomotive is running from a driver and his assistant, the fireman.

6. An evening dinner with some important local factory owners.

His day might start with breakfast, prepared and served by his cook and housemaid (he could afford to employ 1 or 2 servants). He might glance at the newspapers — railways were frequently news in the 19th century. Once at the station, there would be meetings with surveyors, accountants, or officials from the railway company. He would try to find time to talk to his staff. Then there would be letters to dictate, and reports to write.

After a busy day, the station-master must have looked forward to a quiet evening at home with his wife and family. But it was often his duty to attend local social events, public meetings or dinners. His presence there would remind people just how important the railway was to the life of their town.

6

FOOD FOR TRAVELLERS

In the early days of the railways, long-distance travellers often arrived at their destinations tired and hungry. Before the 1860s, there were no sleeping cars on trains, and no dining cars, either. Passengers had to take food with them – no easy task in hot summer weather, when a journey might last a week – or else hope to buy something at crowded station refreshment rooms.

Trains would stop for about 20 minutes to allow people to eat a hurried meal, but stories are told of how unscrupulous refreshment room owners bribed guards to arrange for trains to leave early, so that passengers who had paid for food would not have time to eat it. It could then be re-sold to the next trainload of hungry travellers! Not all station refreshment rooms were like this, of course. Most dealt honestly with their customers, and provided reasonable food day and night.

In the 19th century, people were very concerned about distinctions of money and class and so, like carriages and waiting rooms, the refreshment rooms were divided into 1st, 2nd and 3rd classes. First-class passengers could enjoy, at a price, a four-course meal accompanied by fine wines, served in elegant surroundings. Third-class passengers made do with steaming mugs of tea, slabs of cake and stodgy meat pies, served over the counter and eaten standing up.

Above. **The kitchen** on board the famous Blue Train (see page 40). Here, the chef and his assistants worked in dreadfully cramped conditions to prepare superlative meals for the pampered 1st-class passengers en route for the South of France. At dinner, passengers could expect to choose from a menu of five courses, and to be served with the finest wines.

Left. **This illustration** has been redrawn from an American cartoon, making fun of the panic to purchase and consume food and drink during a limited stop for refreshments. Waiters hurry to serve tea and coffee to tired and thirsty passengers, who must gulp it down as fast as possible in case the train sets off again without them. The train guard stands at the refreshment-room door, pocket-watch in hand, urging the passengers to hurry. You can see him at the far left of the picture.

Right. **Before boarding** their train, these passengers can take advantage of waiter-service, from a mobile trolley of food and drink at an American railway station.

Below. **A 1st-class** passenger restaurant, where wealthier travellers could enjoy a sumptuous meal. The different railway companies prided themselves on their restaurants, which were equipped with specially-monogrammed table linen, china and cutlery, and staffed by the best chefs.

LOCOMOTIVES

All steam engines worked on the same principle, although there were many variations and improvements in design during the 19th century. Water was heated in a boiler by burning an easily-combustible fuel in a furnace, called a firebox. The fuel was usually coal or coke, but, in places like the USA and Canada, where wood was plentiful and coal not always available, wood-burning engines were used instead. The heated water turned into steam. This expanded, and, because it was trapped inside the boiler, greatly increased the pressure inside it. The steam pressure was used to drive pistons, which turned wheels, and these propelled the locomotive along the track.

It was a skilled job to maintain a sufficient head of steam at the correct pressure without wasting fuel or allowing the water to fall below boiling point. Steam pressure was regulated by valves, controlled by levers; these governed the speed of the train. Early locomotives were slow, rarely reaching 25 mph. Most 19th-century locomotives travelled at around 60 mph, although some passengers felt this was dangerously fast. Queen Victoria, for example, insisted that her royal trains should never travel at more than 40 mph, although, unlike the 'Dragon Empress' of China, she did not go so far as to order the execution of railway staff who displeased her.

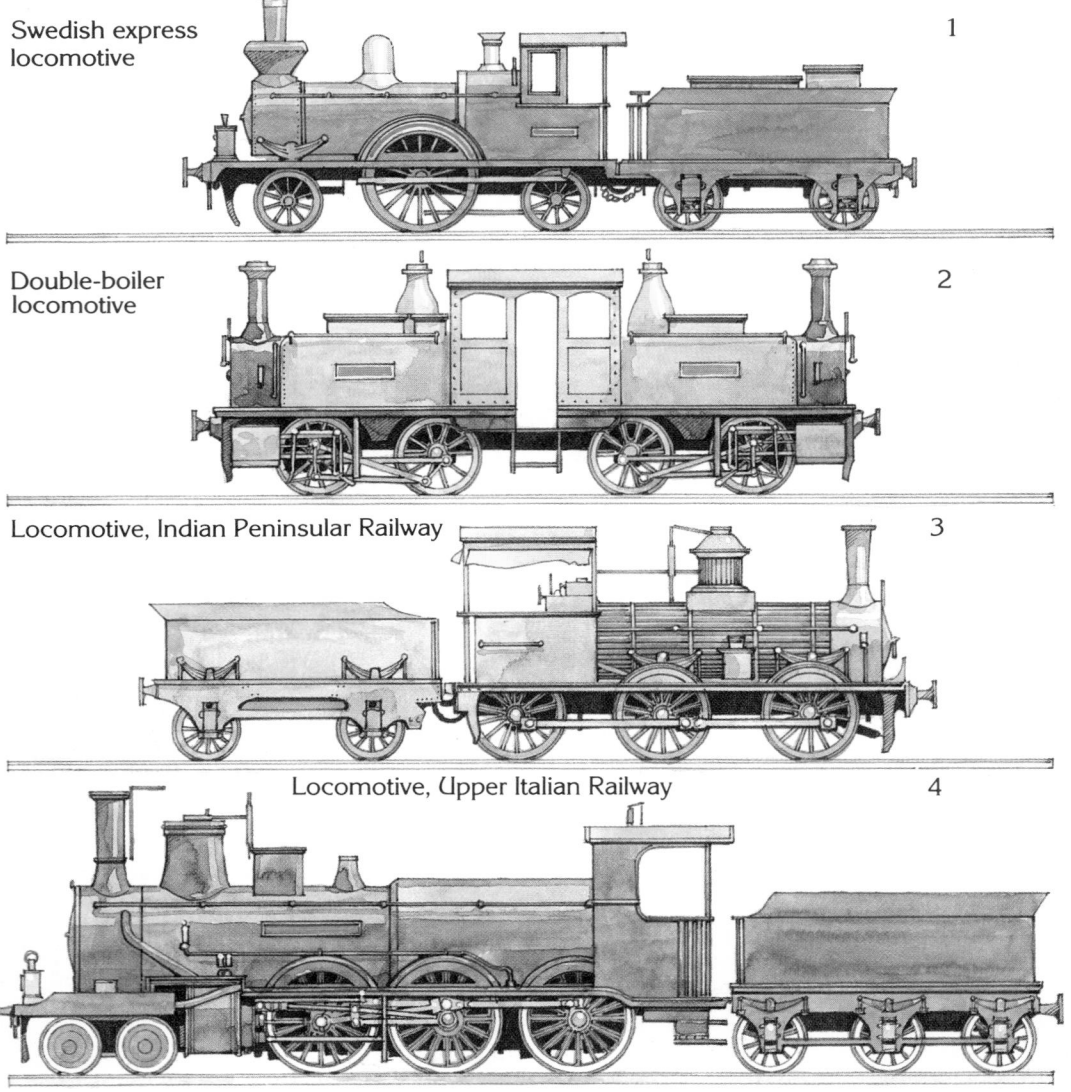

Swedish express locomotive   1

Double-boiler locomotive   2

Locomotive, Indian Peninsular Railway   3

Locomotive, Upper Italian Railway   4

A British engineer, George Stephenson, designed the first successful locomotives. During the 19th century, Britain continued to lead the way in locomotive design, pioneering the building of railways in India, Europe and South America.

1. A small express locomotive operated by Swedish State Railways, 1898. The bulbous base to the funnel is a typically Scandinavian feature; it was designed to trap sparks from the engine, and help to prevent forest fires.

2. A double-boiler, narrow-gauge locomotive, built for use in New Zealand, 1877. Railways played an important part in opening up new, unexplored lands.

3. A massive British-built locomotive, designed for pulling loads up the steep tracks of the Great Indian Peninsular Railway. The first locomotive of this design was built in 1862.

4. An Italian locomotive, designed for use on the Upper Italian Railway (based at Turin) and built in 1884.

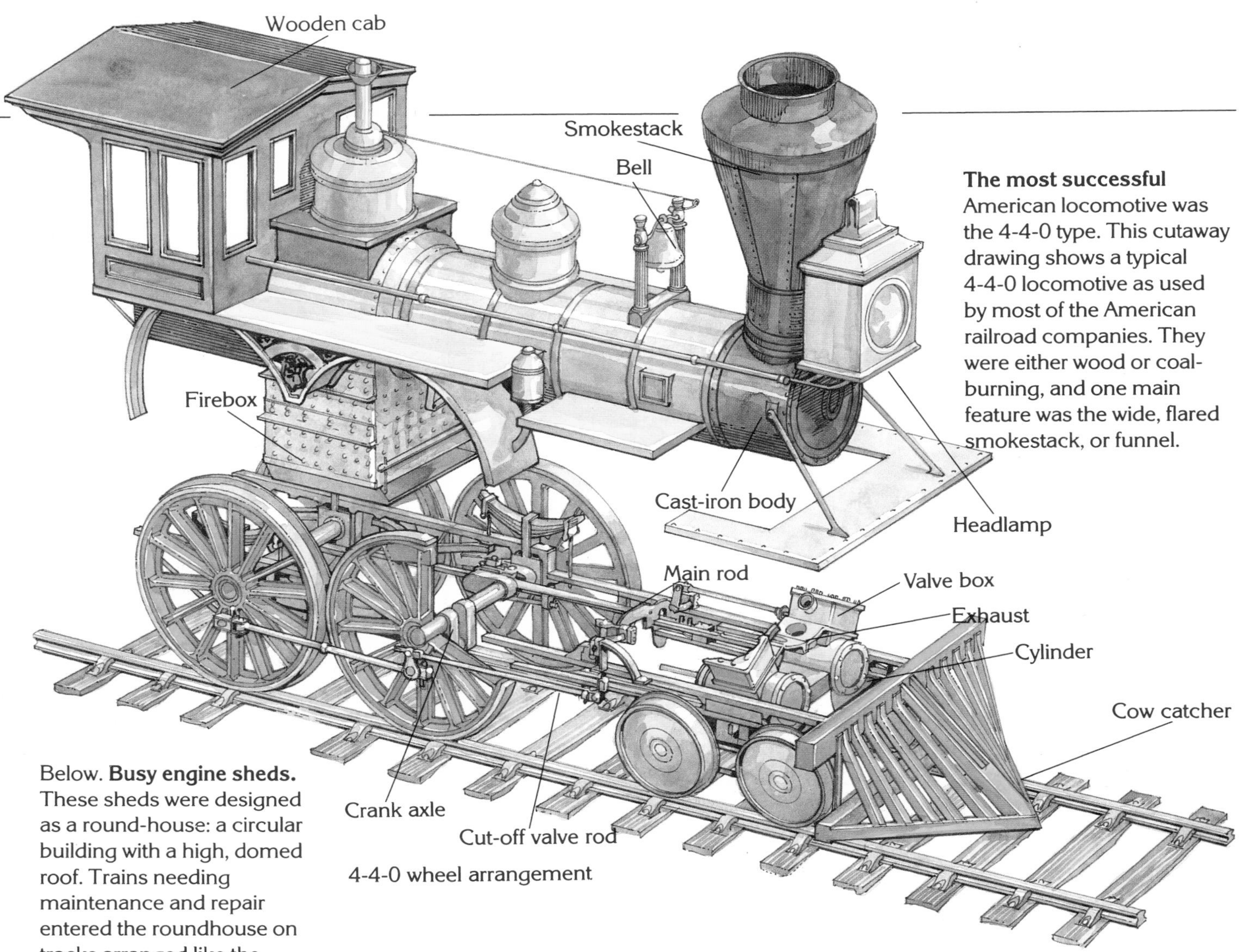

Wooden cab

Smokestack

Bell

The most successful American locomotive was the 4-4-0 type. This cutaway drawing shows a typical 4-4-0 locomotive as used by most of the American railroad companies. They were either wood or coal-burning, and one main feature was the wide, flared smokestack, or funnel.

Firebox

Cast-iron body

Headlamp

Main rod

Valve box

Exhaust

Cylinder

Cow catcher

Below. **Busy engine sheds.** These sheds were designed as a round-house: a circular building with a high, domed roof. Trains needing maintenance and repair entered the roundhouse on tracks arranged like the spokes of a wheel.

Crank axle

Cut-off valve rod

4-4-0 wheel arrangement

Engine sheds

PASSENGER COMFORT

Railways made long journeys possible for large numbers of people in the 19th century, but what were conditions like for passengers? It depended on how much money you were prepared to spend, and also in which country you were travelling. First-class passengers, who paid the highest fares, were offered comfortable padded seats in roomy, nicely-decorated coaches, with wide windows shaded by curtains or blinds, and pictures or ornately-framed mirrors on the walls.

Second-class carriages were crowded, with harder seats, smaller windows, and less decoration, while third-class carriages were extremely simple. The earliest third-class passengers travelled in open trucks, with bare wooden benches to sit on, but by the 1850s roofs were provided. Heated carriages were introduced much later — not until the 1920s on some British trains, although American railway companies installed heating for all classes long before then.

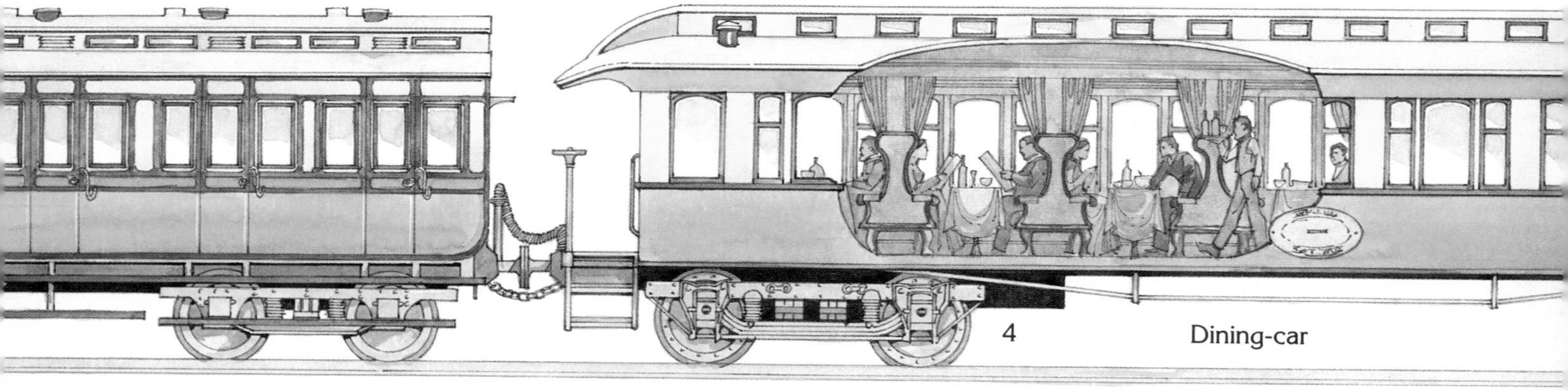

4   Dining-car

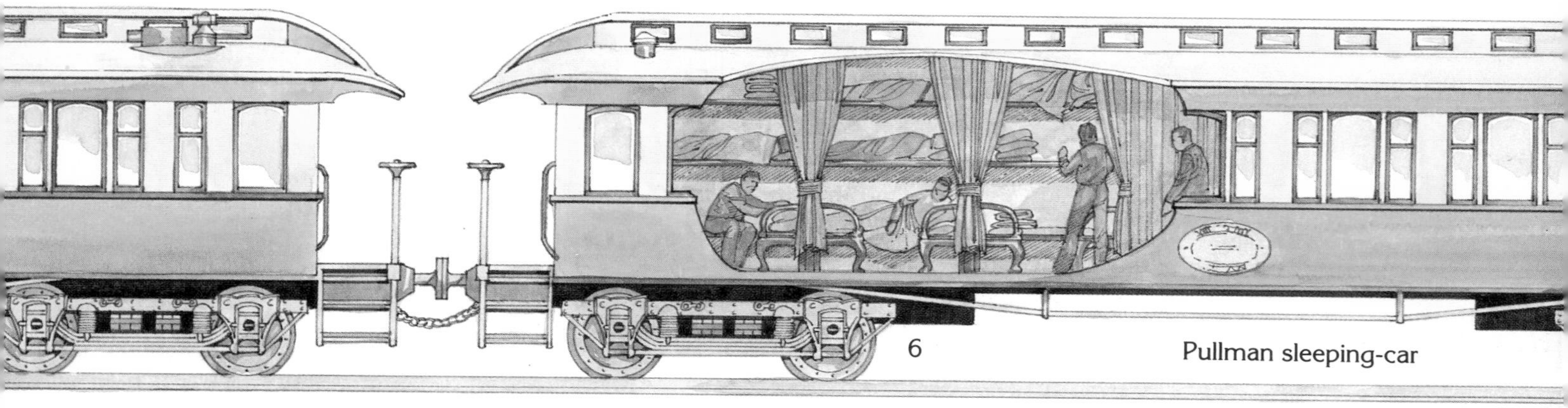

6   Pullman sleeping-car

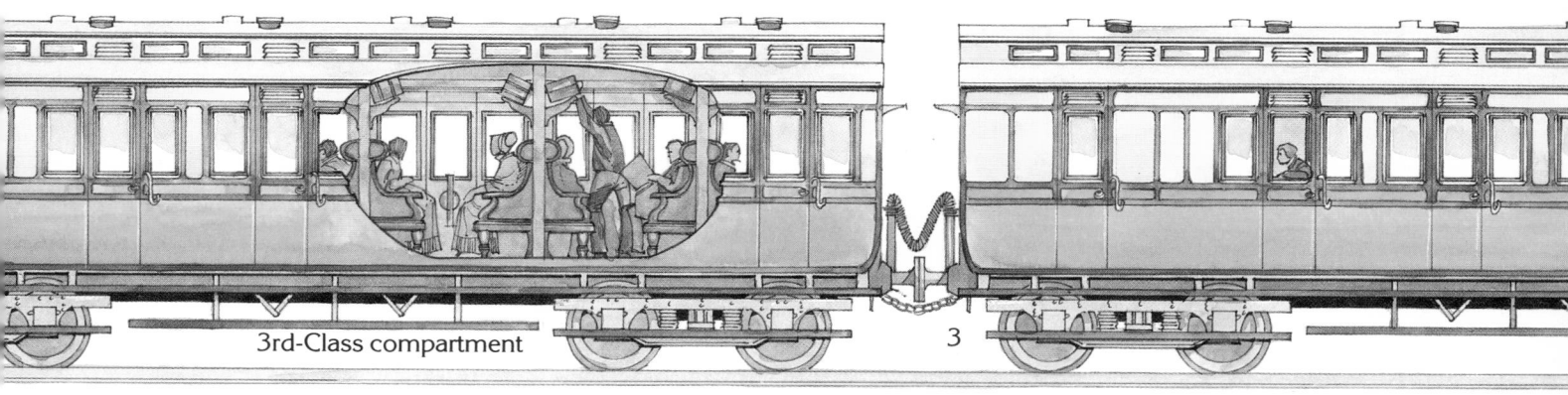

3rd-Class compartment

3

There was another important difference between European and American railway travel. In Europe, early carriages were divided into separate compartments. Once the train was on the move, passengers could not get out until it reached the next station. In contrast, American coaches were designed as a big open-plan saloon; travellers were free to walk about while the train was in motion. This offered less privacy, but was safer; people had been attacked in closed-compartments.

1. By the end of the 19th century, more people were travelling, and for greater distances. Locomotives were designed and built to pull longer, heavier trains, smoothly and efficiently. This locomotive, belonging to the Midland Railway Company, was remarkably elegant and powerful.

2. A 3rd-class compartment, 1875. It has padded seats, ventilation grilles and an overhead lamp. In 1874, the Midland Railway Company abolished its 2nd class, thereby offering more comfortable 3rd-class travel to the majority of its passengers who could not afford 1st-class fares.

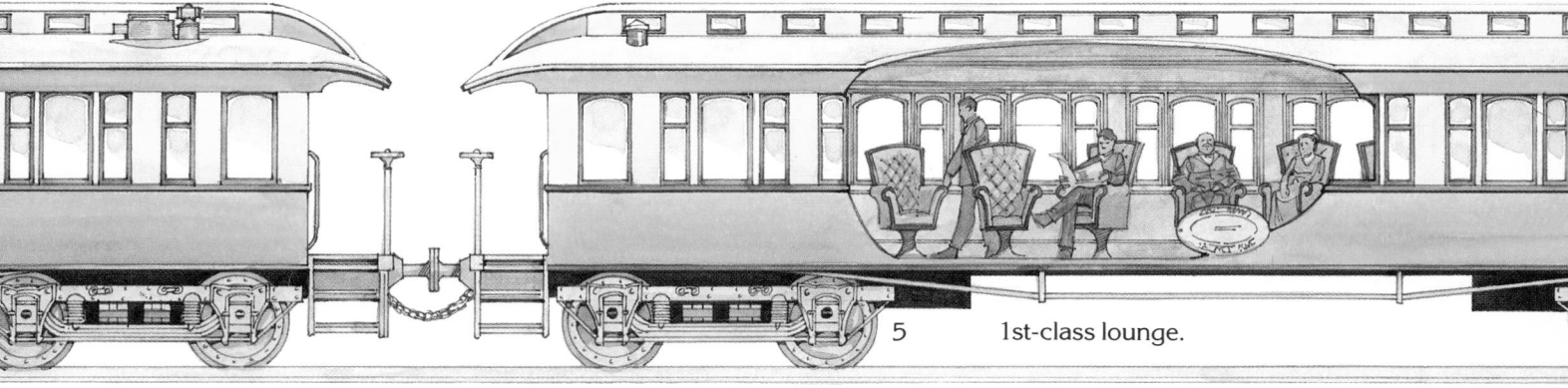

5   1st-class lounge.

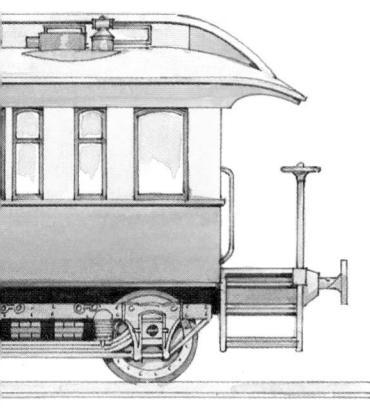

4. A 1st-class dining car, 1906. You can see the silver cutlery and the delicate wine glasses set out on the tables. Passengers would often reserve their seats in coaches like these, and stay comfortably settled in them for the length of their journey.

5. Travellers relaxing in a 1st-class lounge. The lacy covers on the tops of the deep, cushioned armchairs are 'antimacassars', so called because they used to protect the upholstery from a popular hair-dressing (called Macassar oil) used by many men at the time.

6. A Pullman sleeping car (see page 37). Daytime seats can be turned into beds, and a series of bunks let down from the roof. Heavy curtains between each pair of seats give privacy. It cannot have been easy to dress and undress in such a confined space.

LUXURY TRAVEL

In the 1860s, an American, George M. Pullman, had a very unpleasant journey by train. As a result, he declared he would design a coach in which people could 'sleep and eat with more ease and comfort than on a first-class steamer'. Pullman soon won fame as a builder of comfortable railway carriages, and his name is still used today to describe luxurious travelling conditions.

Pullman's new coaches were a considerable

Above. **The first Pullman** dining car in Europe came into service in 1879, on the Great Northern Railway. Copied from American coaches, it was soon very popular with travellers.

The Bavarian Royal Train

Right. **The magnificent** Royal Train, built for King Maximilian II of Bavaria (Germany) in 1860. Probably the most elaborately-decorated train ever; the outside coachwork was brilliant royal blue, and all the carvings were gilded. Larger than life-size crowns ornamented the roof, and there was a balcony at the rear of the carriage, where local dignitaries could be received when the train halted at the station. Inside, there was a saloon with extravagantly-carved chairs and sofas and a solid marble table. Even the toilet seat was padded with swansdown.

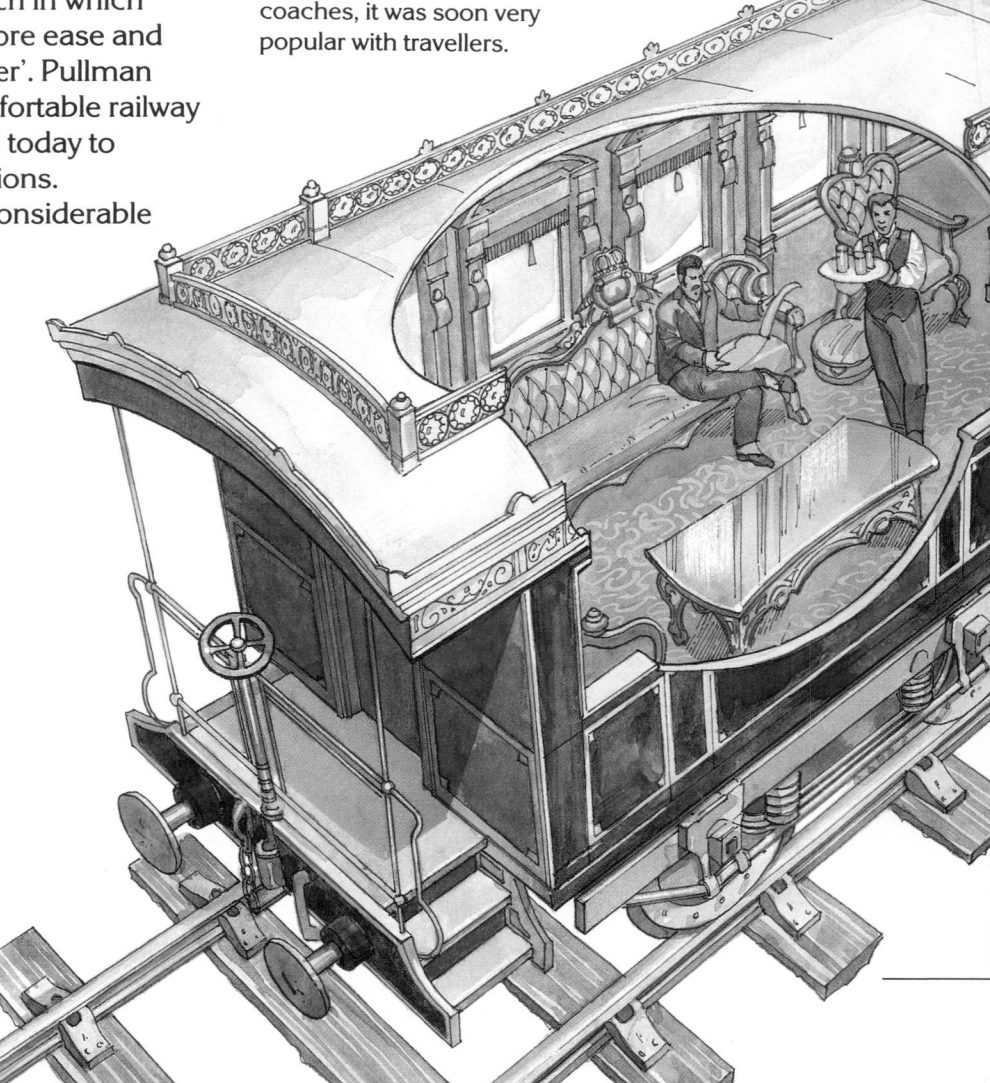

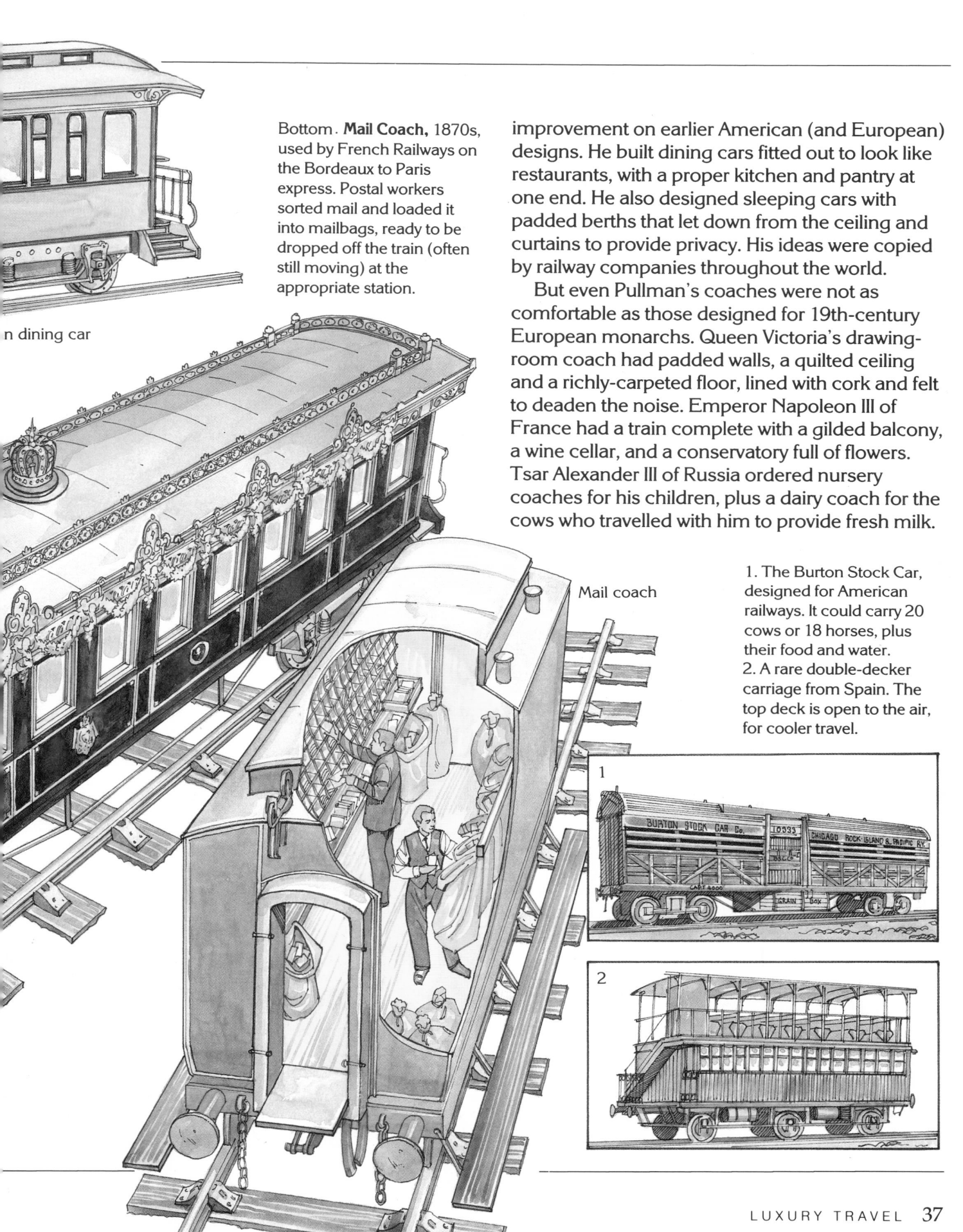

Bottom. **Mail Coach,** 1870s, used by French Railways on the Bordeaux to Paris express. Postal workers sorted mail and loaded it into mailbags, ready to be dropped off the train (often still moving) at the appropriate station.

n dining car

Mail coach

improvement on earlier American (and European) designs. He built dining cars fitted out to look like restaurants, with a proper kitchen and pantry at one end. He also designed sleeping cars with padded berths that let down from the ceiling and curtains to provide privacy. His ideas were copied by railway companies throughout the world.

But even Pullman's coaches were not as comfortable as those designed for 19th-century European monarchs. Queen Victoria's drawing-room coach had padded walls, a quilted ceiling and a richly-carpeted floor, lined with cork and felt to deaden the noise. Emperor Napoleon III of France had a train complete with a gilded balcony, a wine cellar, and a conservatory full of flowers. Tsar Alexander III of Russia ordered nursery coaches for his children, plus a dairy coach for the cows who travelled with him to provide fresh milk.

1. The Burton Stock Car, designed for American railways. It could carry 20 cows or 18 horses, plus their food and water.
2. A rare double-decker carriage from Spain. The top deck is open to the air, for cooler travel.

CHEAP AND CHEERFUL

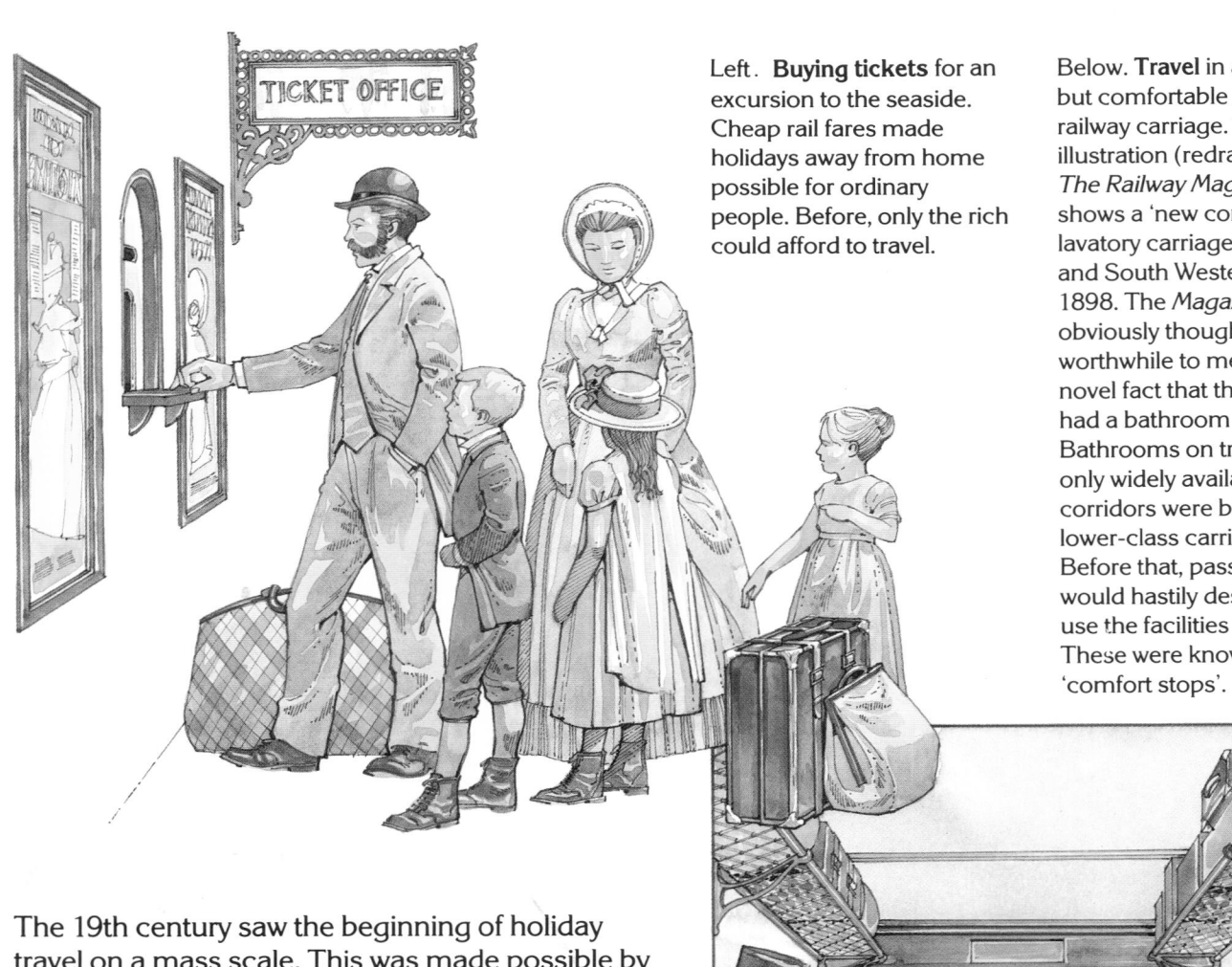

Left. **Buying tickets** for an excursion to the seaside. Cheap rail fares made holidays away from home possible for ordinary people. Before, only the rich could afford to travel.

Below. **Travel** in a simple but comfortable 3rd-class railway carriage. This illustration (redrawn from *The Railway Magazine*) shows a 'new composite lavatory carriage, London and South Western Railway', 1898. The *Magazine's* editor obviously thought it worthwhile to mention the novel fact that this carriage had a bathroom on board. Bathrooms on trains were only widely available once corridors were built in lower-class carriages. Before that, passengers would hastily descend to use the facilities at stations. These were known as 'comfort stops'.

3rd-class carriage

The 19th century saw the beginning of holiday travel on a mass scale. This was made possible by railways; poor people could now afford a trip to the seaside, or to their nearest big city. They knew, too, that it would not take all their precious holiday time to reach their destination. Railway travel brought distant holiday centres to within a day's journey for a great many people.

The first excursion by train was organised by the Nottingham Mechanics' Institute in 1840, to visit an exhibition in Leicester. Soon, go-ahead railway companies began to organise excursions from big industrial cities to resorts in the country or by the seaside. Factory workers who spent most of the year indoors welcomed the chance to escape into the fresh air and sunshine. And the routine of factory work, with its regular annual leave, made it possible for railway companies to predict when the busiest times for travel would be, and to lay on extra trains to cope with the demand.

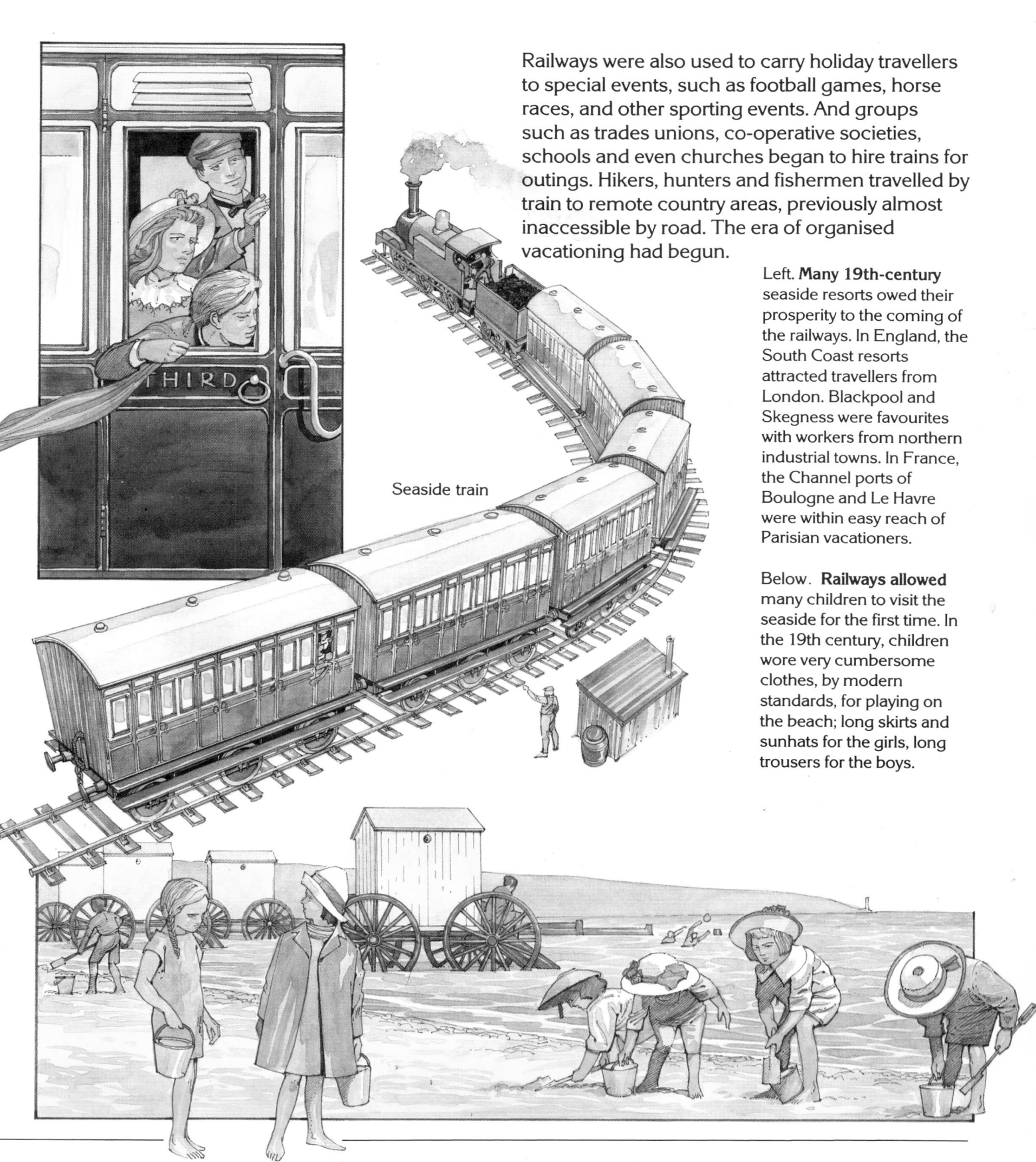

Railways were also used to carry holiday travellers to special events, such as football games, horse races, and other sporting events. And groups such as trades unions, co-operative societies, schools and even churches began to hire trains for outings. Hikers, hunters and fishermen travelled by train to remote country areas, previously almost inaccessible by road. The era of organised vacationing had begun.

Left. **Many 19th-century** seaside resorts owed their prosperity to the coming of the railways. In England, the South Coast resorts attracted travellers from London. Blackpool and Skegness were favourites with workers from northern industrial towns. In France, the Channel ports of Boulogne and Le Havre were within easy reach of Parisian vacationers.

Below. **Railways allowed** many children to visit the seaside for the first time. In the 19th century, children wore very cumbersome clothes, by modern standards, for playing on the beach; long skirts and sunhats for the girls, long trousers for the boys.

Seaside train

THIRD

TRAVELLING IN STYLE

In contrast to the noisy, crowded excursion trains, it was possible to travel in a refined and exclusive style on 19th-century railways. Enterprising companies ran special luxury trains, the most important of which were those developed by Georges Nagelmackers, a Belgian engineer. In 1883, he pioneered an international service, linking Paris – the most sophisticated capital in Europe – with the romantic and mysterious city of Constantinople (now Istanbul), gateway to the exotic lands of Asia and the Middle East.

Journeys on this train, the Orient Express, were immensely expensive ($260 in 1885, or several years' wages for a domestic servant), but they were also fast, safe and very comfortable. The Orient Express soon became popular with wealthy and

One family and their luggage.

glamorous travellers from Europe and America. Nagelmackers followed this success with another luxury service, the Blue Train, which ran from Paris to Nice, an expensive and elegant resort on the warm Mediterranean coast. Like the Orient Express, the Blue Train catered only to the rich. Accommodation was limited to 10 passengers per coach, the restaurant car served exquisite food, and, after dinner, travellers returned to their comfortable sleeping berths, equipped with crisp linen sheets, ample hot water and fluffy towels. It was just like staying in a top-class hotel.

1. The sumptuous 1st-class waiting room at the Gare de Lyon, Paris. Passengers for the famous Blue Train lingered here, under the painted ceilings and sparkling chandeliers.

2. An American Pullman 'Parlor Car', like a cosy sitting room. Not everyone liked this fussy decor; one 19th-century writer called it 'a veritable riot of the worst conceivable ideas'.

3

4

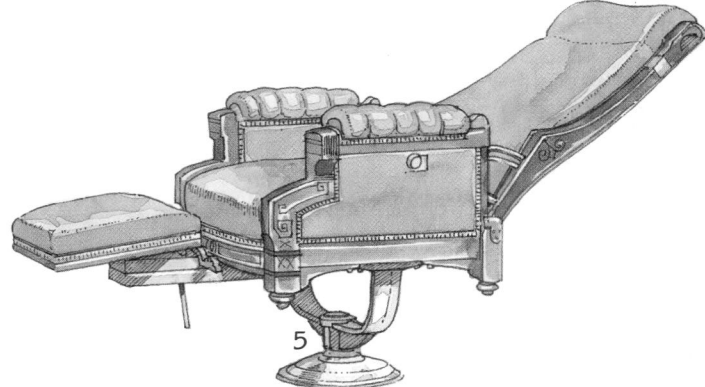

5

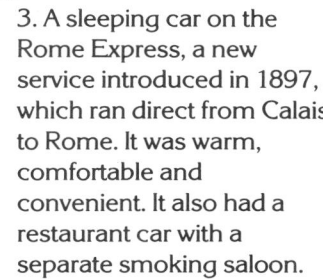

3. A sleeping car on the Rome Express, a new service introduced in 1897, which ran direct from Calais to Rome. It was warm, comfortable and convenient. It also had a restaurant car with a separate smoking saloon.

4. This is how *Harper's New Monthly Magazine*, (an American journal) described a trip on a Pullman car in 1872: 'You take up residence on the train . . . you undress and go to bed as you would at home . . . you sit at little tables . . . you order your breakfast, dinner or supper from a bill of fare which contains a surprising number of dishes . . . admirably cooked . . . You may have a choice in the wilderness of buffalo, elk, antelope, grouse . . .'

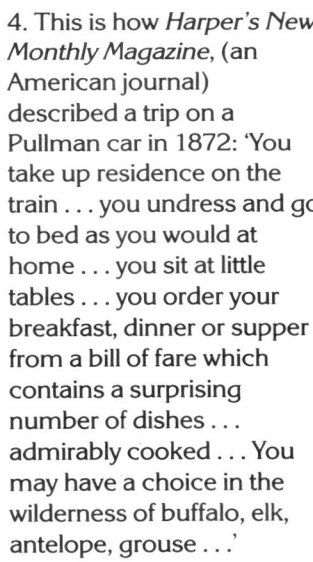

5. A variety of reclining chairs, from the 1880s, introduced on American railroads so passengers could travel comfortably on long journeys.

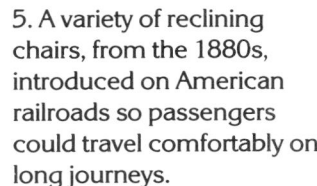
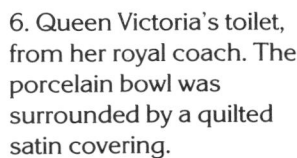

6

6. Queen Victoria's toilet, from her royal coach. The porcelain bowl was surrounded by a quilted satin covering.

FREIGHT ON THE RAILWAYS

Freight yards belonging to the New York Central and Hudson River Railroad Company, c. 1890. In the background, you can see a huge grain elevator, used to store enormous quantities of wheat grown on the Mid-West prairies. In the foreground, locomotives are busily shunting a variety of wagons. Freight trains hauling grain to depots like this were sometimes almost a mile long.

As well as grain, freight trains brought cattle from the West, fruits from California, timber from Michigan, coal from Virginia and cotton from the South to the cities.

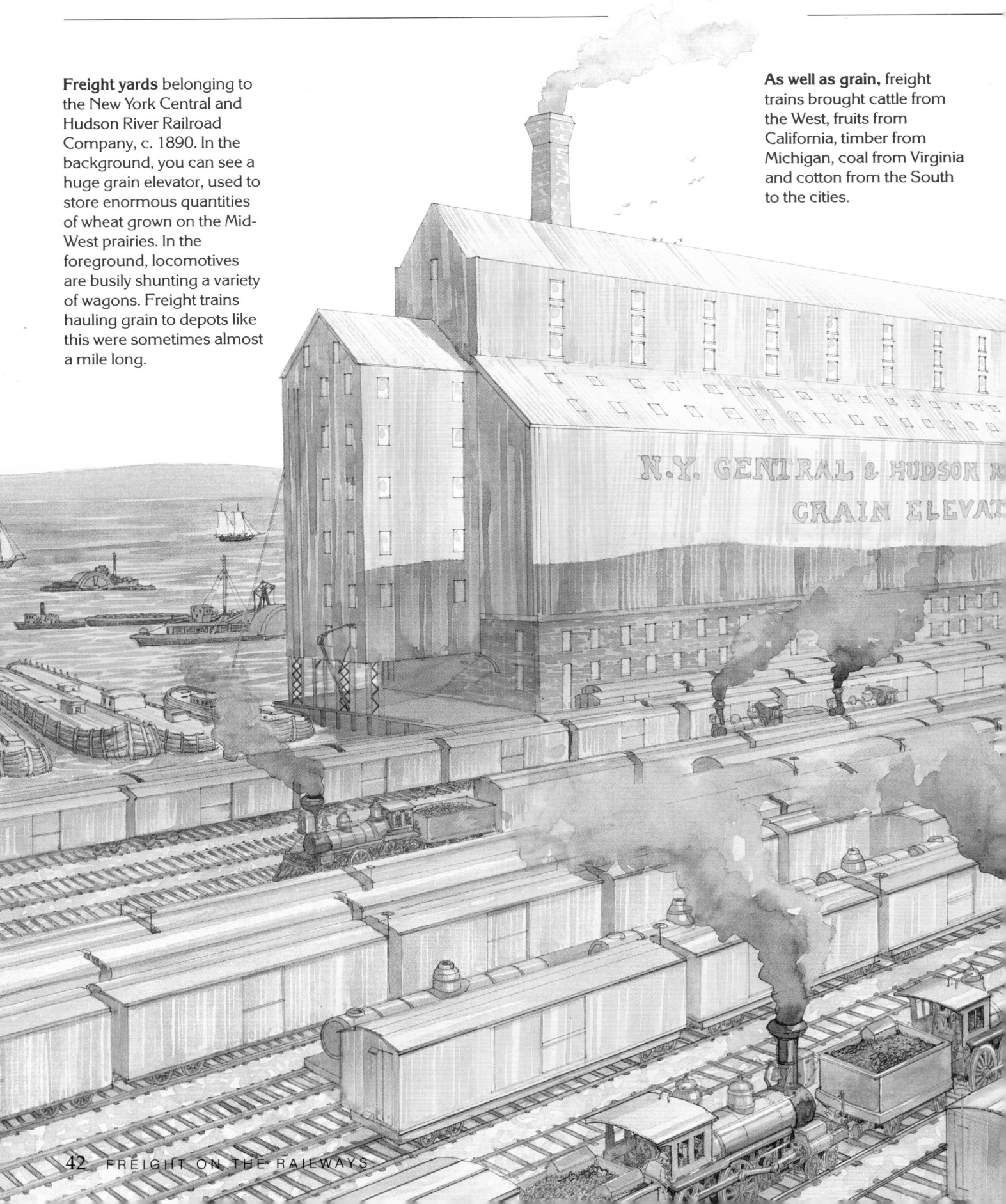

In the 19th century, railways brought the country nearer to the town, and the towns closer together. Without a railway station, towns were cut off from the rapid industrial and commercial developments that were taking place in Europe and America. Sometimes, towns even offered bribes to railway companies encouraging them to build new lines near them, in the hope that they would bring extra trade and greater profits to their shops and factories. In the USA and in Russia, new railway lines brought distant parts of each vast country into contact for the first time ever. This helped fledgling industries based on products from remote areas (such as gold, timber and, later, oil) to develop, and established lucrative new trading links between big cities and distant provinces.

What sort of goods did the railways carry? All sorts of bulky raw materials needed for the rapidly-growing factories — cotton, wool, coal, iron ore, chemicals and building materials — and the many kinds of manufactured goods, including textiles, clothing, household equipment, and also weapons and armaments, that these factories produced. Railways also brought fresh food to city-dwellers. Every morning, churns of fresh milk, crates of vegetables, baskets of eggs, as well as deep-sea fish and fresh meat were carried from country stations or coastal ports to city markets.

Many great seaports were also linked to national railway networks. This enabled goods from overseas to be carried quickly to towns and cities.

Freight yards were sometimes built alongside lakes or rivers; this made it easy for cargoes to be quickly transhipped from wagons to barges.

Goods yards were kept busy, day and night, with trains arriving from far-flung places. Traffic was controlled by a senior railway official known as the yardmaster. He had to know the contents of each wagon, its destination, and which track it had to follow through the maze of points and sidings.

NEW USES FOR OLD STATIONS

Today, many people feel nostalgia for the passing of the 'age of steam', for the mighty locomotives, hissing majestically amid clouds of smoke and showers of sparks, and for the vast, imposing railway stations built to house them and the passengers who travelled by train. It is interesting to compare their feelings with those of a mid 19th-century writer, describing the first time he saw a steam train in the following romantic terms: 'I had seen no sight like that; I have seen nothing to excel it since. In beauty and grandeur, the world has nothing beyond it.'

In the 19th century, when the power and magnificence of steam locomotives seemed likely to last for ever, the railway companies built grand railway stations, also designed to last. But now that many railway lines have been shut down, and many people travel by car or plane instead of by

Rural station, now a family home

Left:
New restaurant in former
19th-century station hall

train, what kind of future can there be for the great 19th-century stations?

On these two pages, you can see how some old railway stations have been converted for new purposes. Since many are large and spacious, they form ideal exhibition halls, museums, or even centres for the performing arts. Smaller, cosier stations have been turned into houses. A few stand sadly derelict. Whatever their uses, 19th-century stations are still part of all our lives.

New uses for old railway stations:

1. Pittsburgh, Pennsylvania. The old main hall of the 19th-century station has been turned into a flourishing restaurant. The iron arches form an attractive background to displays of plants and there is enough space for over a hundred diners.

2. Many small rural stations became redundant when the branch lines which served them were closed in the 1960s, as part of a package of measures introduced in Britain to make railways more profitable. Some disused stations have been converted into houses or workshops. Others have been carefully restored to their original condition by railway preservation societies. Many are open to the public. Old steam locomotives, too, have been rescued by railway enthusiasts and restored.

3. The great 19th-century Paris railway station, the Quai d'Orsay, has recently been turned into a museum devoted to 19th-century art. Its vast spaces (64,000 square yards of floor surface) and high, well-lit glass roof make it ideal for displaying large-scale paintings and sculptures, or holding popular exhibitions. Thousands of people visit it, and it employs a staff of more than 700 people.

4. Malienbaan Station, near Utrecht in the Netherlands. It was built in 1874 and converted in the 1950s into a railway museum.

Musée d'Orsay, Paris

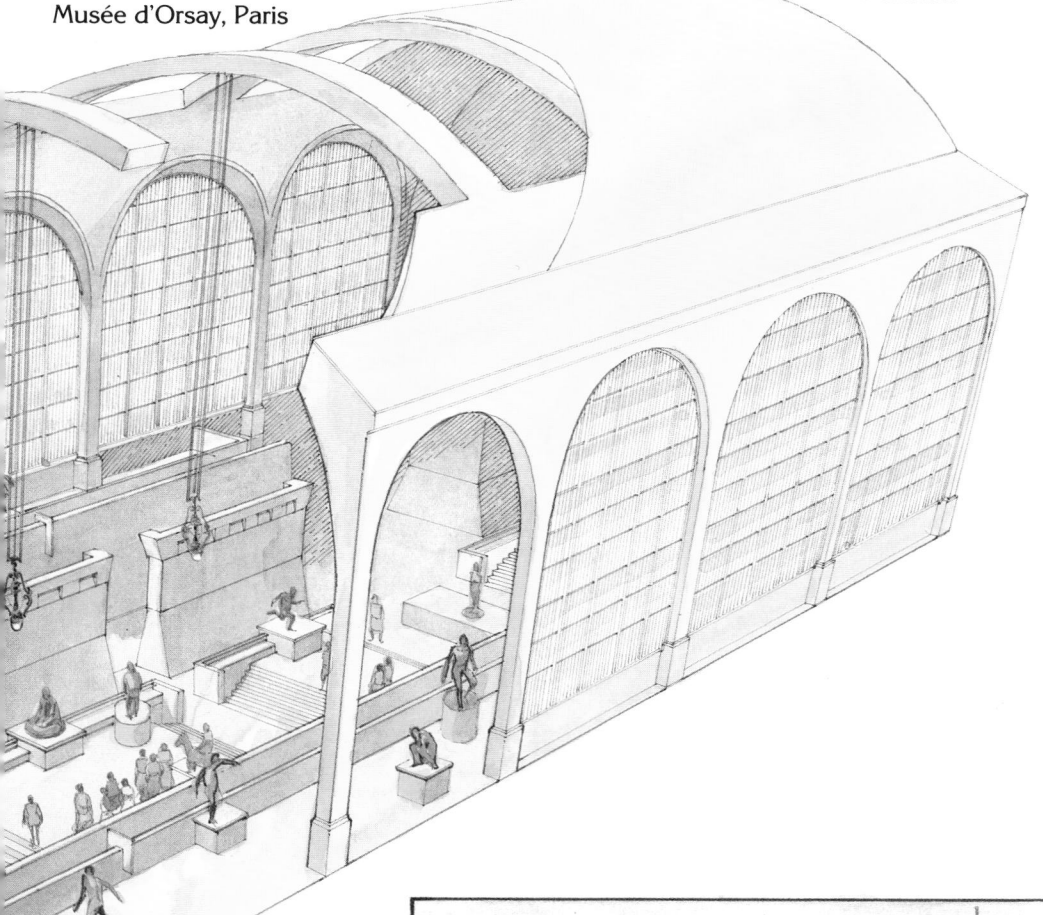

Right: 19th-century station converted to a railway museum

GLOSSARY

Ballast, a layer of solid material — often rock chippings — used to form a secure base on which to lay sleepers (see below) and railway tracks.

Cantilever, a bridge where the main span is supported by a solid structure at one end, which holds the span in place by balancing its weight. Imagine a ruler sticking out from a pile of books: the weight of the books on top of the 'buried' portion of the ruler keeps the projecting portion securely in position.

Cast iron, iron which is heated to a very high temperature until it becomes liquid. It is then poured into different-shaped moulds, where it sets hard as it cools. Nineteenth-century mouldings made from cast iron were often very elaborate; some station roofs and archways looked almost like lace. Cast iron is relatively cheap, and also strong and rigid, but brittle and very heavy. Unlike mild steel (see below) it cannot be hammered or bent into shape.

Chandelier, a large overhead light-fitting, originally designed to hold dozens of candles, but often, by the early 20th century, converted either to gas or electricity.

Commute, to travel daily from home to place of work. People who travelled from the suburbs (see opposite page) into the big cities to work became known as commuters.

Cross-braced, supported by a criss-cross framework.

Embankment, an artificially-constructed bank of earth, usually with sloping sides, raised above the surrounding land. Railway tracks were laid along the top of embankments where the existing terrain was unsuitable for building. Certain great 19th-century railway embankments were several miles long.

Flanged, fitted with a rim, or with another projecting piece of metal. See the drawing on page 20, for flanged wheels on locomotives and railway carriages.

Girder, a strong beam of iron or steel used in the construction of bridges and buildings.

Investors, people who lend money to a company to help finance new projects. In the 19th century railway companies borrowed money from investors to help them build stations. In return, they paid the investors a percentage of any profits they made.

Metropolis, large city.

Mild steel, a type of steel (a mixture of carbon, iron, and small amounts of other metals) that is strong and easily-shaped. It is much lighter and more flexible than cast iron (see above). In the 19th century, it was used, with glass, to build roofs, windows and conservatories.

Monogrammed, decorated with a design of one or more letters, usually initials.

Morse code, a system of signalling using different combinations of 'dots' and 'dashes' (short and long sounds) to represent different letters of the alphabet. In the 19th century, Morse signals were sent by wire, as a series of bleeps or clicks. They were then noted down on paper and translated into words by highly-trained clerks, or else received by a special signalling instrument, which printed out the message.

Pier, a pillar supporting a bridge.

Piston, part of an engine: a metal plunger that fits tightly inside a cylinder, and is connected at one end to a crank linking it to wheels mounted on an axle. As steam (or petrol vapour) pressure increases inside the cylinder, the piston is forced outwards, moving the crank and so turning round the wheels.

Plate glass, glass manufactured in large, thick sheets. Plate glass was a new invention in the 19th century. It enabled buildings to be designed with entire roofs made of glass, or with enormous glass windows. This had not been possible before. Buildings which used a large amount of glass in their construction were much cheaper than traditional brick structures.

Rack-and-pinion, a system used to help locomotives climb steep mountain slopes. On rack-and-pinion railways, locomotives are fitted with toothed cogwheels in between their normal wheels, and an extra line of notched track is laid between the rails. (The cogwheel is the 'pinion' and the extra track is the 'rack'.) As the locomotive moves forward, the teeth on the cogwheel fit into the notches on the track; this stops the train sliding backwards down the slope (which it would otherwise tend to do, because of its weight) and helps to drag it along the upward track.

Redundant, no longer useful.

Rolling stock, a term used to describe all the wheeled vehicles used on railways, including waggons, locomotives, trucks and carriages.

Semaphore, a system of signalling using two 'arms', which can be moved to a variety of positions. Each position has a specific meaning – on 19th-century railways the most common signal messages told the driver to 'stop', 'go', and 'proceed with caution'.

Shunter, a railway workman whose job it was to crawl between trucks and carriages in the sidings (see below) and link them together to form trains. It was hard, dirty work and could be dangerous, sometimes causing injury.

Sidings, the area of the railway tracks close to the station buildings where rolling stock (see above) was kept when not in use. Stations which handled a great deal of goods traffic often had several miles of sidings, where the goods wagons could stand while they were waiting to be loaded or unloaded.

Sleepers, heavy wooden planks, set in ballast (see opposite page) to which railway tracks were fastened. Sleepers were treated with tar to preserve them, but were eventually rotted by damp and frost, and needed to be replaced.

Stucco, a thick plaster-based mixture, which was used in the 19th-century to decorate the outside of some buildings.

Suburbs, areas on the outskirts of towns. In the 19th century, residential suburbs grew up around the edges of many industrial towns, as people moved further away from the noisy, grimy centres in search of pleasanter, more peaceful conditions in which to live.

Track train, a train carrying construction workers to the stretch of railway line they were in the process of building.

Truss, a long, strong beam of wood or metal.

Valve, a device to control pressure. There are numerous different designs for valves, and they have hundreds of different uses. The most important valves on 19th-century locomotives worked by allowing steam from the locomotive's boiler to escape into the atmosphere. This lowered pressure inside the boiler, slowed down the working of the pistons, and reduced the speed of the train.

Viaduct, a tall structure, rather like a bridge, built to carry a road or railway above the surrounding land. Viaducts carried railways across deep valleys, above marshy ground, or even, by the late 19th century, above dingy workers' houses in crowded industrial cities.

Villa, a large, comfortable house.

INDEX